THE LIFE & WORK OF
ROGER BACON

AN INTRODUCTION TO
THE OPUS MAJUS

BY

JOHN HENRY BRIDGES
M.B., F.R.C.P.
SOMETIME FELLOW OF ORIEL COLLEGE, OXFORD

"Induire pour déduire, afin de construire."
AUGUSTE COMTE, *Synthèse Subjective*.

"Omnes scientiae sunt connexae, et mutuis se fovent auxiliis, sicut partes ejusdem totius, quarum quaelibet opus suum peragit, non solum propter se, sed pro aliis." ROGER BACON, *Opus Tertium*.

EDITED, WITH ADDITIONAL NOTES AND TABLES, BY
H. GORDON JONES, F.I.C., F.C.S.

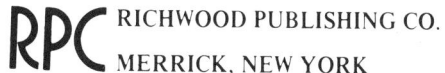

RICHWOOD PUBLISHING CO.
MERRICK, NEW YORK

B
765
.B24
B7
1976
2596361

Published by Richwood Publishing Company
Merrick, New York

Reprinted: 1976
Printed in U.S.A.

Reprinted from the original edition in the
University of Illinois Library.

Library of Congress Cataloging in Publication Data

Bridges, John Henry, 1832-1906.
   The life & work of Roger Bacon.

   Reprint of the 1914 ed. published by Williams &
Norgate, London.
   Includes index.
   1. Bacon, Roger, 1214?-1294. I. Title.
B765.B24B7 1976   189   76-1120
ISBN 0-915172-14-3

THE LIFE & WORK OF
ROGER BACON

EDITOR'S PREFACE

THIS volume is a new edition of the *Introduction* which the late Dr Bridges prefixed to his edition of the *Opus Majus*, published at the Clarendon Press in 1897. The Preface to that edition contains full details as to the important differences between it and the earlier edition of Jebb (1733), but it may be well to point out here two of the principal features of the Oxford edition. (1) It contained for the first time what Jebb had so unaccountably omitted, the important seventh part of the *Opus Majus*, dealing with Moral Philosophy, the crowning portion of the whole work. (2) To his annotated edition of the Latin text Dr Bridges prefixed a most useful analysis in English.

Dr Bridges had already contributed the biography of Bacon to the *New Calendar of Great Men*,[1] and in 1903 he delivered an admirable Lecture before the University Extension Students

[1] Macmillan and Co., 1892.

at Oxford on Roger Bacon. This was published in the volume of *Essays and Addresses*.[1] I have, with the permission of Mrs Bridges, made use of those portions of this Lecture which contain important matter not treated so fully in the *Introduction*, as follows. The shorter extracts from the Lecture have been placed as additional footnotes, while the longer and more important passages will be found in the Appendix at the end of the book. (All such extracts are characterized by the reference *E. and A.*)

Other footnotes, elucidative of various points in the *Introduction*, have been taken from the three volumes of the *Opus Majus*. (These are denoted by the reference *Op. Maj.*) All the additional footnotes, including the editorial ones, have been placed within brackets to distinguish them from Dr Bridges' footnotes to the *Introduction*.

In his Preface to the supplementary volume (1900) of the *Opus Majus*, Dr Bridges said:—

Three motives prompted me, in 1893, to undertake a new edition of Roger Bacon's *Opus Majus*. One was that the sixth centenary of one of the earliest and perhaps the greatest of Oxford thinkers was at hand. A second reason was that this work brings into prominence the connexion of Greek science with that of the modern world, through the mediation of the Arabic schools of

---

[1] Chapman and Hall, 1907.

EDITOR'S PREFACE

Bagdad and Spain. And thirdly, the *Opus Majus*, when published in its entirety, appeared to me to present to the world a scheme of culture contrasting strongly with any that was offered in Bacon's time or in the centuries that followed. Combining the comparative study of language with a comprehensive grasp of physical science, conceiving these studies as progressive, and yet holding them subordinate to a supreme ethical purpose, it surpassed any that was put before the world till the publication of the philosophical and social works of Auguste Comte.

In my selection of the additional notes to this edition I have been guided by a consideration of Dr Bridges' aims as set forth in the above statement, and I think it will be found that this supplementary matter emphasizes and brings into still greater prominence both the standpoint of Dr Bridges in this subject and the true nature of Bacon's work.

The compendium of 'Facts Relating to Bacon's Life,' which appears in vol. i of the *Opus Majus*, has been reproduced here, and I have added a Table of the Seven Parts of the *Opus Majus*, also a Table of the *Scriptum Principale*, to enable the reader to see more clearly the general scheme of each of those works.

The English Positivist Committee now issue Dr Bridges' *Introduction* in a separate form, on the occasion of the seventh centenary of the birth of Roger Bacon, in the belief that it constitutes the most adequate general estimate of the Life and Work of the great Franciscan in our language, and with the hope that by so doing a much wider circulation may be obtained for it than has been hitherto possible.

H. GORDON JONES.

January 1914.

CONTENTS

	PAGE
EDITOR'S PREFACE	5
TABLE OF FACTS RELATING TO BACON'S LIFE . .	11
SECTION I. BACON'S LIFE	13
,, II. BACON'S POSITION IN THE METAPHYSICAL CONTROVERSIES OF THE THIRTEENTH CENTURY . . .	41
,, III. BACON'S *SCRIPTUM PRINCIPALE* .	54
,, IV. BACON'S PHILOLOGY	62
,, V. BACON'S MATHEMATICS . . .	75
,, VI. BACON'S ASTROLOGY	83
,, VII. THE PROPAGATION OF FORCE . .	93
,, VIII. BACON'S OPTICS	101
,, IX. BACON'S ALCHEMY	112
,, X. EXPERIMENTAL SCIENCE . . .	120
,, XI. MORAL PHILOSOPHY	122
,, XII. GENERAL CHARACTERISTICS OF THE *OPUS MAJUS*	138

APPENDIX

NOTE	PAGE
A. ROBERT GROSSETESTE	146
B. ARISTOTLE AND THE UNIVERSITY OF PARIS	149
C. TABLE OF THE SEVEN PARTS OF THE *OPUS MAJUS*	151
D. ,, ,, *SCRIPTUM PRINCIPALE*	152
E. BACON'S GEOGRAPHY	153
F. THE THREE PREROGATIVES OF EXPERIMENTAL SCIENCE	157
G. THE MATHEMATICAL AND EXPERIMENTAL METHODS	161
H. A SUMMARY OF PARTS I–VII OF THE *OPUS MAJUS*	162
I. BACON AS A CATHOLIC	166
J. THE MOHAMMEDAN SCHOOLS OF LEARNING	167
INDEX OF PROPER NAMES	169

TABLE OF FACTS RELATING TO BACON'S LIFE

Contemporary events.	Statements resting on later authority.	Facts verified by Bacon's statement or by contemporary authority.
1209. Condemnation of Aristotle's *Physics* and *Metaphysics* in Paris. **1215.** Confirmation of this by Papal Legate. (Cp. *Op. Tert.*, cap. 9.) **1222.** Alexander of Hales enters the Franciscan Order, and teaches philosophy in Paris. **1231.** Condemnation of *Physics* and *Metaphysics* partially removed by Gregory IX. **1238.** Alexander of Hales resigns his post as a teacher of philosophy. **1245-8.** First residence of Thomas Aquinas in Paris with Albertus Magnus. **1249.** Death of William of Auvergne (Bishop of Paris). **1252.** Second residence of Aquinas in Paris of uncertain duration. **1253.** Death of Grosseteste. **1256.** Bonaventura becomes General of Franciscans. **1258.** Bagdad captured from Saracens by Tartars. **1265.** Guy Fulcodi elected Pope Clement IV. **1268.** Death of Clement IV. **1270.** Death of Saint Louis.	*c.* **1214.** Born near Ilchester in Somerset, or, according to another tradition, in the parish of Bisley in Gloucestershire. (*Cf.* Brewer, p. lxxxv.) **1240.** Went from Oxford to Paris about 1240. Probably entered Franciscan Order a few years later. **1250-7.** Probably in Oxford. Legend as to Bacon's Tower may perhaps be referred to this period.	**1230.** Michael Scot introduces his translations of Aristotle. (*Op. Maj.*, vol. i, p. 55.) **1233.** Interview of Bacon with Henry III at Oxford, as described by Matthew Paris. **1245.** Heard William of Auvergne (Bishop of Paris) lecture on *intellectus agens*. (*Op. Tert.*, cap. 23.) **1250.** Saw the leader of the Pastoureaux marching through France in 1250. (*Op. Maj.*, vol. i, p. 401.) **1257.** 'Exile' from Oxford to Paris began. (*Op. Tert.*, cap. 1.) **1258-67.** His family took the King's side in war with barons. (*Op. Tert.*, cap. 3.) **1264-5.** Enters into relations with Guy Fulcodi. **1266.** Bacon ordered to send his writings to the Pope.

Contemporary events.	*Statements resting on later authority.*	*Facts verified by Bacon's statement or by contemporary authority.*
1274. Death of Bonaventura; Jerome of Ascoli becomes General of Franciscans. Death of Thomas Aquinas. **1280.** Death of Albertus Magnus. **1288.** Jerome of Ascoli becomes Nicholas IV; Raymundo Galfredi succeeds him as General. **1292.** Death of Nicholas IV.	**1278.** Imprisonment *propter novitates suspectas,* 1278. (See *Summa Historialis* of Antoninus, Archbishop of Florence, a writer of the fifteenth century.) **1292.** Release from prison probably 1292. Died 1292 or 1294. Buried in Franciscan Church in Oxford. Legend as to exposure of his writings to wind and weather told by Wood.	**1266-7.** Composition of *Opus Majus, Opus Minus, Opus Tertium.* **1268.** Death of Clement IV. **1271.** Writes the *Compendium Studii Philosophiae,* denouncing the corruptions of the Church. (See Brewer, p. liv.) **1292.** Writes *Compendium Studii Theologiae.* See MS. of this work (Br. M. Royal 7 F. vii, fol. 78).

THE LIFE AND WORK OF ROGER BACON

I. BACON'S LIFE

IN considering the little that is known of the life of Bacon, it is well to give precedence to the few facts that are fixed with perfect precision by his own statement. We know with entire accuracy the date of the composition of the *Opus Majus*,[1] and of the two subsidiary works, the *Opus Minus* and the *Opus Tertium*. Pope Clement IV's[2] in-

---

[1] ['The title *Opus Majus* is not found in the work itself. But as the treatise is continually spoken of by this name in the *Opus Tertium* it is convenient to preserve it here.'—*Op. Maj.*, vol. iii, p. 159.]

[2] Guy Fulcodi (or Foulques), who succeeded to the Papacy in 1265 as Clement IV, was born at Saint Gilles in Languedoc. He began his career by studying law, in which he achieved great distinction. He was married and had several children. He seems to have acted for some time as a private secretary to Louis IX. After his wife's death he entered the Church, was made archbishop of Narbonne in 1259, and cardinal bishop of Sabina in 1261. (See Fleury, *Hist. Eccl.*, liv, 85, whose spelling of the name Guy Fulcodi is here adopted.) Brewer conjectures

structions to him to transmit the results of his labours were issued June 22, 1266, from Viterbo. Within the year that followed, the *Opus Majus*, with its supplement, the *Opus Minus*, and its introduction, the *Opus Tertium*, had been completed and sent to the Pope. At this time he speaks of himself as an old man, and he says that he had been studying language, science, and philosophy for nearly forty years (*Op. Tert.*, cap. 20). From this it may be supposed that he was born between 1210 and 1215. But the place of his birth cannot be said to be fixed with certainty.

One, and only one, notice of his name occurs in a contemporary writer. Matthew Paris relates, under the year 1233, that Henry III convoked the counts and barons of the kingdom to a council

(pp. xi *et seq*.) that he entered into relations with Bacon on the occasion of his mission to England as Papal legate in 1263 or 1264. But Bacon was then in Paris, and had been there for several years. Guy Fulcodi had far better opportunities of hearing about Bacon in Paris than could have occurred during the time of his stormy and ineffectual legation to England. ['In 1266 a letter reached Bacon from the Pope requiring him to send him a fair copy of his writings, all orders to the contrary from his superiors notwithstanding; ordering him at the same time to set down in writing what were the remedies proposed for the dangers of which he had spoken. From this letter, which is preserved in the Papal archives, where I have myself seen it, it appears that Bacon had already put himself in communication with Clement, both before and after his elevation to the Papacy.' —*E. and A.*, p. 177.]

at Oxford. Their animosity against Pierre des Roches, Bishop of Winchester, the king's chief adviser, who had surrounded his person with a body-guard of Poitevins and filled England with these foreigners, led them to refuse the summons. While the king was debating what measures to take against the recalcitrant barons, a Dominican preacher, Robert Bacon by name, told him frankly that there would be no hope of permanent peace in the kingdom so long as the Bishop of Winchester and his son, or kinsman, Peter of Rievaulx, retained power. Robert Bacon's opinion was echoed by others, and the king was induced to listen to it patiently. 'Then a certain clerk who was present at the Court, Roger Bacon by name, a man of mirthful speech, said with pleasant yet pointed wit, " My lord king, what is that which is most hurtful and fearful to those that sail across the sea?" "Those know it," the king replied, " who have much experience of the waters." " My lord," said the clerk, " I will tell you; stones and rocks"; meaning thereby Pierre des Roches.' It has been thought that the date of the dialogue was too early to refer to the Roger Bacon with whom we are here concerned. But since he might well be more than twenty years old at the time, the doubt seems hardly founded.

What is certain from Bacon's own statement is

that his family was one of some wealth, since he himself had been able to spend much money on experimental research. It appears also that this family had taken the royal side throughout the disputes between Henry and his barons, and had suffered pecuniary loss and exile for their loyalty. He tells Pope Clement that, being in sore distress for the money necessary for the transcription and conveyance of his MSS., 'I wrote to my brother, a rich man in my country. But he, belonging as he did to the king's party, was in exile with my mother, brothers, and the whole family. Ruined and reduced to utter poverty, he was unable to help me, and up to the present day he has sent me no reply.' (*Op. Tert.*, cap. 3.)

The forty years of study, of which he speaks in 1267, may be divided into two periods, apparently of nearly equal length; the periods before and after his admission into the Franciscan Order. In the seventeenth chapter of the *Opus Tertium* he speaks of having devoted more than twenty years to the study of languages and of science. 'I sought,' he says, 'the friendship of all wise men among the Latins; and I caused young men to be trained in languages, in geometrical figures, in numbers, in the construction of tables, in the use of instruments, and in many other necessary things. . . . During this time I spent more than two thousand pounds in those things and in the purchase of books and instruments.' We may presume that the pounds were French, which at that time would correspond to between 600 and 700 pounds sterling. The sum was a large one. And whether large or small, it would be quite incompatible with the profession of an Order specially devoted to poverty. It may be inferred, therefore, that since he had studied independently for some twenty years, it was not till some time between 1245 and 1250 that Bacon became a Franciscan.

Among the men distinguished for their learning whose friendship he cultivated at this part of his career may be counted, in all probability, Adam Marsh ; Edmund Rich, afterwards Archbishop of Canterbury and ultimately canonized ; Thomas Bungay, whose name was one day to be associated with his own as a worker of magic ; Thomas, Bishop of St Davids ; John of Basingstoke, scholar and traveller ; John Peckham, afterwards Archbishop of Canterbury ; Hermann, one of the principal translators of Aristotle ; Shirwood, the treasurer of Lincoln ; and last and greatest, the illustrious Bishop of Lincoln, Robert Grosseteste. In Bacon's earlier years of study, Grosseteste had not plunged into the arduous and absorbing work of his episcopate. *Novit scientias*, Bacon says of him. He was *rector scholarum*, and also Chancellor of Oxford, and in 1224 was the rector of the Franciscans recently established there. The terms in which Bacon bears testimony to his encouragement of philology, to his attempts to apply mathematical method to the study of physical phenomena, to his disregard of the philosophy of the schools as founded on bad translations of Aristotle (*Comp. Stud. Phil.*, Brewer, cap. 8), would be conclusive as to his personal contact with this great man, even though it were not confirmed by reference to Grosseteste's scientific writings, in which Bacon's debt to him is unmistakable. His treatise *De Physicis Lineis, Angulis, et Figuris* contains passages as to the spherical radiation of force, and as to the change in its direction by reflexion and refraction, which bear a close resemblance to the language used many years afterwards by Bacon.[1]

It would appear that, at the beginning of the thirteenth century, there was a stronger impulse towards scientific study in Oxford than in Paris. In the eleventh chapter of the *Opus Tertium*, when speaking of the science of Optics, Bacon observes, 'On this science no lectures have as yet been given in Paris, nor anywhere among the Latins, except twice at Oxford.' It is not stated that the

[1] [See Note A (Robert Grosseteste) on p. 146.]

BACON'S LIFE

lecturer was Grosseteste; but we may well believe it. It may be supposed that the influence of Adelard of Bath,[1] the first translator of Euclid, had left its traces. Twenty years before the close of the twelfth century we hear of two Englishmen, Alexander Neckham and Alfred of Sershall, lecturing in Paris on the *Physics* of Aristotle, then recently introduced from the school of translators from Arabic directed by Archbishop Raymond of Toledo.

But the University of Paris, placed nearer the centre of the spiritual forces that swayed mediæval society, had grown up under the dialectical influences of theological controversy; and when Bacon went there, perhaps about 1240, he found what is called, vaguely and inaccurately enough, the scholastic philosophy in the fullness of its growth, with the enlarged scope given to it by the recent permission to study the *Physics, Meta-*

[1] ['The writer referred to is Adelard of Bath, who lived in the early part of the twelfth century. He fills an important place in the history of mediæval science. He was the first translator of Euclid into Latin; not, however, from Greek but from Arabic. A more complete translation was made in the following century by Campanus. (See Weissenborn, *Abhandlungen zur Geschichte der Mathematik*, Drittes Heft, Leipsic, 1880, pp. 141-166.) Adelard studied in the schools of Tours and Laon; and subsequently travelled in Greece and Asia Minor. In Bacon's mathematical treatise, as yet unpublished, he is frequently mentioned, always under the name Alardus. (See Sloane MSS. 2156, ff. 74-97.)'—*Op. Maj.*, vol. i, p. 6 *n.*]

physics, and *Psychology* of Aristotle.[1] Its two most prominent representatives were at this time Alexander of Hales and William of Auvergne. Of the methods and the controversies then current Bacon made himself a master, and received the title of doctor. To be able to speak the language of the schools with authority was the first condition of obtaining a hearing. But he was not slow to perceive that the men who taught this philosophy were, for the most part, wholly destitute of positive knowledge. They knew no language but Latin. Beyond the shreds of arithmetic, mensuration, and astronomy taught in the manuals of the Quadrivium, they were ignorant of mathematics. Of the possibility of applying mathematical knowledge to the facts of nature they had formed no conception whatever. Their philosophy was a tangle of barren controversies reducible, for the most part, to verbal disputes. It bore no relation to the facts of real life. It held out no hope of raising the Catholic Church to the position of intellectual domination needed for establishing her authority over the Asiatic world, from which dangers were looming of appalling magnitude.

It was in Paris that Bacon came into contact with a remarkable man of whom very little would

[1] [See Note B (Aristotle and the Univ. of Paris) on p. 149.]

BACON'S LIFE

be known to us but for Bacon's eulogies, Peter of Maricourt,[1] a native of Picardy. From the description given of him in the thirteenth chapter of the *Opus Tertium*, he would seem to have been an unambitious man, anxious only to pursue his researches in private, regardless of the metaphysical turmoil around him. Speaking of experimental research, Bacon says: 'One man I know, and one only, who can be praised for his achievements in this science. Of discourses and battles of words he takes no heed: he follows the works of wisdom, and in these finds rest. What others strive to see dimly and blindly, like bats in twilight, he gazes at in the full light of day, because he is a master of experiment. Through experiment he gains knowledge of natural things, medical, chemical, indeed of everything in the heavens or earth. He is ashamed that any things should be known to laymen, old women, soldiers,

[1] There is some doubt as to the orthography of the name, though none can now be left as to the identity of the person indicated. Émile Charles (pp. 17-18) mentions a MS. in the Paris Library (Bibliothèque Nationale, Manuscrits Latins, 7378) in which the only known work of Peter Peregrinus is spoken of as 'Epistola Petri Peregrini de Maricourt ad Sygerium de Fontancourt, militem, de Magnete.' Charles adds that there is a village called Mehariscourt in Picardy near the abbey of Corbie. The Latin form of the word in one MS. of the *Opus Tertium* is written Maharncuria, but in others Mahariscuria. *Cf.* vol. ii, p. 203 *n.*, of the *Opus Majus*; see also Bertelli's *Declinazione Magnetica* (Rome, 1892).

ploughmen, of which he is ignorant. Therefore he has looked closely into the doings of those who work in metals and minerals of all kinds; he knows everything relating to the art of war, the making of weapons, and the chase; he has looked closely into agriculture, mensuration, and farming work; he has even taken note of the remedies, lot-casting, and charms used by old women and by wizards and magicians, and of the deceptions and devices of conjurers, so that nothing which deserves inquiry should escape him, and that he may be able to expose the falsehoods of magicians. If philosophy is to be carried to its perfection and is to be handled with utility and certainty, his aid is indispensable. As for reward, he neither receives nor seeks it. If he frequented kings and princes, he would easily find those who would bestow on him honours and wealth. Or, if in Paris he would display the results of his researches, the whole world would follow him. But since either of these courses would hinder him from pursuing the great experiments in which he delights, he puts honour and wealth aside, knowing well that his wisdom would secure him wealth whenever he chose. For the last three years he has been working at the production of a mirror that shall produce combustion at a fixed distance; a problem which the Latins have neither solved nor attempted, though books have been written upon the subject.'

Of this remarkable man little is known but what Bacon tells us in the foregoing and other passages of the *Opus Tertium*, and the *Opus Majus*. But what we know is not inconsistent with Bacon's eulogy. Libri, in a note contained in the second volume of his *Histoire des sciences mathématiques en Italie*, transcribes the letter written [1269] by Peter Peregrinus of Maricourt to a certain Sigermus of Fontancourt,[1] which is a treatise on the properties of the magic stone, on the relations of its poles to those of the heavens and earth, on the way to find these poles; on the repulsion in two magnets of poles of the same name, and the attraction of those of different names; and on the construction of a [magnetic] globe which should revolve with the revolution of the heavens, and thus supply the place of the ordinary observation by the astrolabe. This is, no doubt, the invention of which Bacon speaks in the sixth part of the *Opus Majus*.[2] Gilbert, in his great work on Magnetism,[3] makes frequent mention of this treatise

[1] [See the preceding footnote.]
[2] [The motion of the globe was to be effected by magnetic forces.]
[3] [*De magnete, magneticisque corporibus, et de magno magnete tellure*, 1600.]

of Peter Peregrinus; and a careful comparison of the two works, separated as they are by an interval of more than three centuries, shows undoubted and weighty obligations of Gilbert to his predecessor. In the construction of globular magnets (the 'terrella,' or model of the earth), in the mode of finding their poles, the procedure, and indeed the very language of Peter, is closely followed by the later inquirer.[1]

To a mind so original as Bacon's, trained in scientific method by Grosseteste and other members of the English mathematical school, the influence of an experimental thinker like Peter of Maricourt must have been stimulating in the extreme. Bacon was thirsting for reality in a barren land infested with metaphysical mirage. From the horse-load of verbal controversies contained in the *Summa* of Alexander of Hales, from the interminable series of tedious commentaries on Aristotle, of which so great a master as Albert was setting the first fatal example, he took refuge in the visions of the harvest of new truth that was to be reaped by patient observation of nature,

[1] [For a full account of Peter's treatise on the magnet and a most interesting description of his remarkable inventions, such as that of the pivoted compass with divided circle, see S. P. Thompson's *Petrus Peregrinus de Maricourt and his Epistola de Magnete.* (*Proc. Brit. Acad.*, vol. ii, 1906.)]

by submission of her processes to experimental questioning, by following the lowly paths used by plain men in their daily avocations. 'The wiser men are,' he said, 'the more humbly will they submit to learn from others; they do not disdain the simplicity of those who teach them; they are willing to lower themselves to the level of husbandmen, of poor women, of children. Many things are known to the simple and unlearned which escape the notice of the wise. . . . I have learned more important truth beyond comparison from men of humble station, who are not named in the schools, than from all the famous doctors. Let no man therefore boast of his wisdom, or look down upon the lowly, who have knowledge of many secret things which God has not shown to those renowned for wisdom' (*Op. Maj.*, vol. i, p. 23).

Assuming that Bacon entered the Franciscan Order about 1247, he would be at that time still in Paris. The degree of doctor of theology, rarely conferred before the age of thirty-five, was probably received about the same time. He tells us (*Op. Tert.*, cap. 23) that he heard William of Auvergne lecturing to the University on the 'active intellect.' This must have been before 1249, the date of William's death. We know that he must have been still in France in 1250, for in that year the revolt of the Pastoureaux[1] broke out; and Bacon tells us that he 'saw their leader walking barefoot in a troop of armed men carrying something in his hands with the care with which a man carries a sacred relic' (*Op. Maj.*, vol. i, p. 401).

For some time between this date and 1257 he was probably in Oxford. Whether he lectured there publicly we do not know. But that he incurred the suspicion of his superiors in the Franciscan Order is certain; whether by audacity in speculation, by experiments looked upon as magical, or by frank exposure of the ignorance of professorial magnates, cannot be said with certainty. His old friends and teachers, Edmund Rich and Adam Marsh, had passed from the scene. Grosseteste, his revered master, was dead, or died (1253) shortly after his return, in despair at the corruption of the Papacy, and half doubting whether Rome had not become the seat of Antichrist. No one was left to promote the study of Greek, which for aught we know died out in Oxford till Erasmus witnessed its revival. In 1256, John of Fidanza, better known as Bonaventura, became General of the Franciscan Order, a man of exalted and aspiring mysticism, eager to revive the spirit of St Francis, and not likely to care much for new

[1] [The Shepherds' Crusade.]

learning that might lead he knew not whither. Perhaps it was by his direction that Roger Bacon, about 1257, was removed from Oxford, and placed under close supervision in the Paris house.

What degree of restriction was placed upon his liberty is not very easy to define with precision. He was not forbidden to write, although he implies that he had not availed himself of the power to do so to any considerable extent. To multiply books by copyists was impracticable; first, because copyists outside the Order could not be trusted to make an honest use of the copies at their disposal; and secondly, because a strict prohibition was laid down and enforced against communicating any manuscripts to those who were not members of the Order. When Pope Clement's message reached him requiring him to transmit his works with the least possible delay, these works for the most part were still unwritten. Nevertheless there were exceptions. He had compiled, he tells us, from time to time, certain chapters on various subjects at the instance of friends (*Op. Tert.*, cap. 2). Among these chapters is probably to be reckoned the treatise *De Multiplicatione Specierum*, which was sent to the Pope by the same messenger who conveyed the *Opus Majus*, though it does not, strictly speaking, form a part of that work. Careful examination shows it to be a portion of the more complete philosophical treatise[1] to the completion of which Bacon always aspired, till the time came, ten years afterwards, when his philosophical career was fatally arrested. Its style is different from that of the other three treatises, *Majus*, *Minus*, and *Tertium*. It is not like these a *Persuasio*, that is, a more or less popular discourse addressed to a reader like Clement IV; a reader of keen understanding doubtless, but at the same time the busiest man in Christendom. The *Multiplicatio Specierum* is a fragment of a systematic work written with full observance of philosophic language and of the dialectic of the schools.

Whatever the discipline imposed during this period of his life, one important sphere of activity undoubtedly remained open to him. For many years he had been striving to form a school of young men, who should carry on the work which he had begun. We have seen in the treatise which throws so much light on the details of his life (*Op. Tert.*, cap. 17), that he had been engaged for a long time in instructing young men in languages, in geometry, in arithmetic, in the construction of tables, and in the use of scientific instruments. From this part of his work he was evidently not cut off during his life in Paris from 1257 to 1267.

[1] [The *Scriptum Principale*.]

BACON'S LIFE

The messenger whom he selected to convey his manuscripts to Pope Clement was a poor lad [John] whom he had been training in this way for five or six years. On the whole it seems probable that the restrictions placed on his liberty at this period of his life were not of extreme severity.

Of the reception given to Bacon's manuscripts in Rome we know absolutely nothing.[1] A few months after their arrival Clement IV died; and the papal see remained vacant for three years. The Pope elected in 1271 (Gregory X) was a Franciscan. Owing his elevation to St Bonaventura, he was not likely to show favour to a suspected member of his Order. Yet it was in this year or shortly afterwards that Bacon wrote the work known as *Compendium Studii Philosophiae*,[2] an introductory discourse, perhaps, for the encyclopædic *Scriptum Principale*, at the completion of

---

[1] ['On the whole, it will be hard to find in the history of literature a work the authenticity of which rests on a sounder foundation. These, and other questions of a more doubtful kind, would be at once disposed of, could the original MS. sent in 1267 to Rome be discovered. But of this there is little hope. We have no knowledge that the work ever reached Pope Clement. In whichever of the many stages between Paris and Rome it may have been detained, it probably did not survive the condemnation which, as we now know from an Assisi document, was passed on Bacon and his works ten years afterwards.'— *Op. Maj.*, vol. iii, pp. xiv-xv.]

[2] Contained in Brewer's work, pp. 393-519.

which he was always aiming. In this treatise Bacon plunged into stronger invective against the intellectual and moral vices of his time than he had ever used before. In no previous writing had the moral corruption of the Church, from the court of Rome downwards, been so fiercely stigmatized; 'the whole clergy is given up to pride, luxury, and avarice. Wherever clergymen are gathered together, as at Paris and Oxford, their quarrels, their contentions, and their vices are a scandal to laymen.' Unbridled violence among kings and nobles, fraud and falsehood among tradesmen and artificers, were the inevitable result. Progress in wisdom was hopeless when the moral condition of those who should promote it was so far below that of the teachers of the pagan world. Unless sweeping remedies were applied by a reforming Pope, there was no prospect but the advent of Antichrist in the near future (Brewer, pp. 399–404).

Perhaps even these denunciations roused less antagonism than the sweeping attacks on the scholastic pedantry of his contemporaries, their false conceit of wisdom, and their preference of metaphysical subtleties and verbal strifes to the pursuit of real knowledge. Of these charges his previous writings had been full, but they were now renewed and emphasized. Aristotelian study,

BACON'S LIFE

which at the beginning of the century had been the great stimulant of thought, was already becoming the great obstruction, and was preparing for the next century a reign of darkness. Based on false and ignorant translations, it were better, Bacon said, to do away with it altogether than that it should be carried on by men ignorant of the language in which Aristotle wrote, and destitute of the scientific training which alone could qualify them for explaining him (Brewer, pp. 469-473).

The storm of indignation had long been gathering: and in 1278 it broke. In that year Jerome d'Ascoli, who four years before had succeeded Bonaventura as General of the Franciscan Order, held a chapter in Paris. Bacon was summoned on account of 'certain suspected novelties.' He was condemned, and thrown into prison.[1] What were the 'novelties' that constituted his crime we do not know. His works abounded in them. It

---

[1] ['We learn from the chronicle of the twenty-four Generals preserved at Assisi (Assisi MS. 329, f. 109a) that Jerome "by the advice of many of the brothers condemned and denounced the doctrine of Roger Bacon the Englishman, master of theology, containing certain suspicious novelties; for which the said Roger was condemned to prison, with order given to all the brethren that none should hold his doctrine, but avoid it as reprobated by the order. He wrote, moreover, to the Lord Pope Nicholas III, so that by his authority this perilous doctrine might be altogether silenced."' —*E. and A.*, p. 180.]

was not perhaps difficult to show that he had gone too far in connecting changes in religious faith with conjunctions of Jupiter and Mercury; and in hinting that underneath the jugglery of the magicians, valuable truths might sometimes lie concealed. The real motives for stifling his voice lay far deeper.

That he should have held the history of Greek philosophy to have been under the keeping and guidance of Providence no less than the history of Judæa; that he should have regarded the teaching of the Stoics on personal morality as superior to that of any Christian teacher; that he should have dwelt with such frequent emphasis on the ethical value of Mohammedan writers like Al-Farabi, Avicenna, and Al-Ghazali—these were things likely to startle even the most tolerant and thoughtful of his contemporaries, much more the common average of his Order, who had suspected him of unsound views for twenty years. Not indeed that his career would have been impeded by the fact that the founder of the Franciscans had shown disregard, if not dislike, of worldly knowledge. Alexander of Hales had joined the brotherhood before the death of St Francis, and had dominated the schools of Paris long before the voice of Albert had been heard there, and while Aquinas was a child. To a man of ordinary temper, addicted to bold speculation, the protection of so powerful a corporation as the Franciscans had become when Bacon joined them would have been invaluable. But Bacon threw his chances away. He attacked the celebrities of his own Order as severely as those of its rival. His fiery and impatient spirit was to be bound by no shackles of prudence. He had come to Paris fresh from the teaching of men like Grosseteste, eager for the promotion and diffusion of science, no less than for the reform of the Church. He found the great university immersed in dialectical controversy. Many of the controverted questions were of momentous importance, and Bacon was prepared to take his part in them. But they were prosecuted by men devoid of scientific training, unprepared therefore to distinguish truth from error, verbal subtleties from fundamental realities; unwilling even to take the trouble to study Aristotle and the Bible in their original language. He saw that philosophy without science could not fail to degenerate (as history, ancient and modern, shows that it always has degenerated) into academic pedantry, and would confirm that one of the aberrations of intellect which he looked on as the worst and the most fatal, the false conceit of knowledge. Against ignorance under the cloak of wisdom he urged, like Socrates, a lifelong war ; and, like Galileo, he met with a worse fate than that of Socrates, the martyrdom of enforced silence.

No crusade has been conducted by blameless crusaders. It cannot be denied that Bacon's indiscriminating zeal included, with pedants and obscurantists who were his lawful prey, two men who were his equals, one of them, perhaps, his superior. Albert was a student of nature as well as a philosopher. Aquinas, as a student of man and of society, and as the constructive thinker who gave coherency to the vast fabric of Catholic discipline, achieved results which, judged at the distance of six centuries, Bacon neither equalled nor approached. Jealousy of the rival Dominican Order, of which these men were the chief ornaments, cannot account for Bacon's failure to recognize their value ; for the Irrefragable Doctor, Alexander of Hales, was a Franciscan, and was criticized more harshly than either. In their failure to appreciate duly the importance of scientific culture as a basis of Catholic action on a doubting and unbelieving world, the doctors of the Paris schools were all alike involved in his unmeasured strictures. We may understand, though we cannot justify, his impatience. He has bitterly expiated it by many centuries of neglect.

It can hardly be doubted that the seclusion

consequent on his condemnation in 1278 was effective and rigorous. Appeals to the Pope had been anticipated by Jerome, who took care to impress on the court of Rome the expediency of confirming his decision. All hopes of completing the *Scriptum Principale* were shattered. He remained a prisoner, so it is thought, for fourteen years. Jerome meantime had become Pope Nicholas IV. After his death in 1292, a chapter of the Franciscans was held in Paris, at which Raymund Gaufredi, then General of the Order, set free some of those who had been condemned in 1278. It may be looked upon as nearly certain that Bacon was of the number. Certain at least it is from his own words that in that year he was again at work, on his last treatise, the *Compendium Studii Theologiae*, in which the date 1292 is expressly mentioned. Whether he died in this year, or two years afterwards, is uncertain. He was buried in the Franciscan church in Oxford.

The legend that his works were nailed to the walls of the library and allowed to perish ignominiously may be dismissed. But that his lifelong efforts to establish a Catholic school of progressive learning utterly failed, there can be no doubt whatever. Such men as Rich, Grosseteste, and Bacon were not seen at Oxford in the fourteenth century. Greek, mathematics, and experimental science were overwhelmed in the paralyzing mists of Scotian dialectic. Nevertheless it would be an error to suppose that his life-work was a failure. Here and there throughout Europe the tradition of the Doctor Mirabilis survived as a stimulating force, and kept the embers of scientific study alive till the time of the Renaissance.

In proof of this, three instances may be given:—

1. Pierre d'Ailly, in his *Imago Mundi*, written early in the fifteenth century, discussing the relations of the extreme east and west of the habitable globe, has a long passage treating of the probable proximity of Spain and India. For all that appears in the work this passage is his own. But in fact it is a verbal quotation from the fourth part of the *Opus Majus* (vol. i, pp. 290-1).[1] And it has a history worth recording. For it is cited in 1498 in a letter from Columbus to Ferdinand and Isabella, as one of the authorities that had put it into his mind to venture on his great voyage.[3]

---

[1] ['In this celebrated passage [2] Bacon insists that the habitable portion of the globe extends much farther to the east, and also much farther to the south than is commonly supposed; and that the interval between the west of Spain and the eastern extremity of Asia is far smaller than Ptolemy imagined.'—*E. and A.*, p. 173.]

[2] [It occurs in the geographical sub-section; for an account of Bacon's Geography see Note E on p. 153.]

[3] ['See *Imago Mundi*, cap. 8; and Humboldt, *Examen Critique de l'histoire de la géographie*, vol. i, pp. 61-70 and pp.

BACON'S LIFE

2. John Dee, in a memorial addressed to Queen Elizabeth in 1582 on the reformation of the Calendar, speaking of those who had advocated this change, says :[1] 'None hath done it more earnestly, neither with better reason and skill, than hath a subject of this British Sceptre Royal done, named as some think David Dee of Radik, but otherwise and most commonly (upon his name altered at the alteration of state into friarly profession) called Roger Bacon : who at large wrote thereof divers treatises and discourses to Pope Clement the fifth (*sic*) about the year of our Lord 1267.[2] To whom he wrote and sent also great volumes exquisitely compiled of all sciences and singularities, philosophical and mathematical, as they might be available to the state of Christ his Catholic Church.' Dee proceeds to give extracts from Bacon's works in proof of these assertions;

96-108; also *Cosmos*, vol. ii, p. 621 (Bohn's ed.). Humboldt remarks that the *Imago Mundi* " exercised a greater influence on the discovery of America than did the correspondence with the learned Florentine Toscanelli."'—*Op. Maj.*, vol. i, p. 290 *n*.]

[1] Dee's memorial is contained among the Bryan Twyne MSS. in Corpus Christi College, Oxford. The supposition that Roger Bacon changed his name on entrance into the Franciscan Order appears to rest on no authority but that of John Dee's very erratic imagination.

[2] [See on this subject the *R. Grosseteste* (1899) of F. S. Stevenson, who shows on pp. 47-8 that Bacon was largely indebted to Grosseteste for his views on the unreformed Julian Calendar.]

and remarks that Paul of Middelburg, who was much occupied with the question of the Calendar, and had treated of it in his work *Paulina de recta Paschae celebratione* (1513), had made great use of Bacon. 'His great volume is more than half thereof written (though not acknowledged), by such order and method generally and particularly as our Roger Bacon laid out for the handling of the matter.' When we remember that it was Paul of Middelburg by whom Copernicus was urged with a view to this very problem to construct more accurate astronomical tables, we shall gladly acknowledge that here, too, Bacon's labour was not lost.[1]

3. No part of Bacon's work was more frequently transcribed than his *Perspectiva*. Based as it was upon the great work of Alhazen, which was itself

[1] ['That the length of the year was wrongly given in the Julian Calendar must have been known to the small group of Arabian men of science who studied Ptolemy's *Almagest*. But that the amount of the error was not matter of common knowledge half a century after the *Opus Majus* was written, is shown by the passage in Dante (*Paradiso*, xxvii. 132–3), where the error is spoken of as being the hundredth part of a day. The difference between $\frac{1}{100}$ and $\frac{1}{130}$ is considerable to those who know Dante's minute and precise way of dealing with such questions. The mean length of the equinoctial year is 365^d, 5^h, 48^m, 46^s. What Bacon showed was that the Julian Calendar made the year too long by the $\frac{1}{130}$ of a day, and therefore in the thirteenth century was ten days wrong.'—*Op. Maj.*, vol. i, p. 270 *n.*]

a development of the *Optica* of Euclid and Ptolemy, and claiming indeed to be but an abridgment or condensation of the truths laid down by his predecessor with wearisome copiousness, it was in fact much more than this. It selected from a mass of propositions, many of them mere displays of geometrical ingenuity, precisely those which aimed at the interpretation of nature, and at the adaptation of the laws of luminous radiation to human purposes. He was aware of what was unknown to Ptolemy and Alhazen, the concentration of parallel rays from reflecting surfaces formed by revolutions of a conic section; though how far he was indebted for this knowledge to Peter Peregrinus or to Vitello cannot be stated with certainty. Of the magnifying powers of convex lenses Bacon had a clear comprehension. He imagined, and was within measurable distance of effecting, the combination of lenses which was to bring far things near, but which was not to be realized till the time of Galileo.

In 1614, a few years after the invention of the telescope, Combach, professor of philosophy in the University of Marburg, published this great work of Bacon, 'viri eminentissimi.' It would be interesting to know whether the allusion in the *Novum Organum* (lib. i. 80) to the work of an obscure monk ('monachi alicujus in cellula') has reference to this work. The *Cogitata et Visa* was written before Combach's edition was published; but examples of the *Perspectiva* were numerous, and it can hardly have been unknown to Francis Bacon. In any case it must have been known to Descartes, to whose epoch-making researches on Dioptrics it assuredly contributed a stimulating influence. This at least they have in common, that light is looked upon as correlated with other modes of propagation of force through the Ether.

With the scientific Renaissance of the sixteenth century, Roger Bacon's name slowly emerged from the darkness which had enwrapped it for three centuries. Astrologers like Dee, Heyden, and Allen hailed him as a champion of their outworn creed. Men of greater mark and sounder judgment, like Selden and Mead, were struck by his emancipation from the pedantry of the schools, and by his forecasts, made at so remote a time, of an age of industrial and scientific discovery. His central aim, the enlistment of progressive intellect in the cause of moral and religious renovation, was appreciated by none. But since the publication of his principal work in the eighteenth century, his name has gradually ascended towards its permanent position, on the lofty summits which were the earliest to 'take the morning' of European thought.

II. BACON'S POSITION IN THE METAPHYSICAL CONTROVERSIES OF THE THIRTEENTH CENTURY

It is too often forgotten that Bacon was a schoolman; trained in scholastic methods, and ready to take part in the philosophic discussions which interested his contemporaries. It is not perhaps surprising that this side of his work should have been ignored; for in the *Opus Majus*, though visible enough to an attentive reader, it is thrown into the shade by the prominence given to positive science, and by the practical application of science to political and religious purposes. Some chapters [38-52] of the *Opus Tertium*, which supplement too hasty or imperfect treatment in the larger work, afford better illustrations of Bacon's aptitude for metaphysical discussion. Nevertheless, the position of Bacon in the scholastic controversies of the thirteenth century remained an unknown quantity till the appearance of Professor Charles's monograph.[1] His comprehensive survey of Bacon's unpublished works includes a careful

[1] [*Roger Bacon*, 1861.]

study of, and copious extracts from, the important fragment of the *Scriptum Principale*, entitled *Communia Naturalium*,[1] of which copies exist in the Mazarine library in Paris and in the British Museum.

Hauréau's comprehensive *Histoire de la Philosophie Scolastique* has made it easy to refute the illusion, still, however, not entirely dissipated, that scholasticism implies a special set of philosophical tenets or an uniform method of treatment. Philosophical writers in the thirteenth century differed from one another no less than philosophical writers in the nineteenth; though in either case a certain similarity in the subjects considered, and in the mode of handling them, was impressed by the circumstances of the time. Scholastic philosophy means simply philosophy taught in mediæval schools. And between the schools of the twelfth, of the thirteenth, and of the fourteenth centuries, there were great and essential differences.

To pass from the reading of the *Policraticus* of John of Salisbury, who knew nothing of Aristotle but his Logic, and that imperfectly, to a treatise of Albert or of Aquinas seems, and is, a transition quite as abrupt as to exchange a volume of

---

[1] [This work has now been published, as follows :—*Communium Naturalium Fratris Rogeri.* Parts I-IV. Ed. R. Steele. Clarendon Press, Oxford, 1909-11.]

POSITION AMONG SCHOOLMEN 43

Addison or Swift for one of Schopenhauer or Carlyle. In the one case as in the other, a tide of revolution had swept between the centuries. For it was nothing less than a revolution for the western mind to receive very suddenly from the Mohammedan world the results of three centuries of Arabian learning, including as it did all the more serious part of Aristotle's work, enriched with keen-witted and audacious comment, and accompanied by the scientific results of the schools of Alexandria ; the *Syntaxis* of Ptolemy and the biology of Galen.

Isolated thinkers like Adelard of Bath, the first translator of Euclid into Latin, had already entered this field of study, when Raymond, archbishop of Toledo, established in the middle of the twelfth century a systematic school of translators from the Arabic, of whom the Jew, Joannes Avendeath (otherwise known as Johannes Hispalensis), Dominicus Gundisalvi, archdeacon of Segovia, the translator of Al-Ghazali, and Gerard of Cremona, best known by his translations of the *Almagest* and of Alhazen, were the most prominent representatives.[1] Their translations of Aristotle, including his *Physics*, *Metaphysics*, and

[1] See Jourdain, *Recherches critiques sur l'âge et l'origine des traductions Latines d'Aristote*, pp. 107–124 (ed. 1843). The history of mediæval translations from Greek into Arabic, some-

Psychology, were not long in finding their way across the Pyrenees. Alexander Neckham, afterwards abbot of Cirencester, lectured upon them in Paris in 1180. His junior contemporary and countryman, Alfred of Sershall, pursued a similar course. Neither of these men roused suspicion. But the case was far otherwise with David of

times through intermediate Syriac versions, and from Arabic into Latin, deserves more elaborate treatment than it has yet received; provided always that the writer of such a history combined the two conditions so constantly insisted on by Bacon: knowledge of the languages concerned and knowledge of the subjects treated. Meantime much useful preliminary work has been done in this direction by such writers as Wuestenfeld and Jourdain. ['Cantor, in his *Gesch. der Mathematik*, speaking of the school of translation set up at Toledo in the twelfth century under the direction of Raymond, the archbishop of that city, by Dominicus Gundisalvi and John of Seville, remarks: "Their labours were conducted in a circuitous fashion which had its consequences. The Arabic was first translated into Castilian, and from this the Latin version was made. Bearing in mind that the Arabic text was taken from the Greek by men whose powers of translation were not wholly beyond suspicion, we may imagine what sort of Aristotelian philosophy reached the mediæval student after three repetitions of bungling."—Cantor, vol. i, p. 684. Jourdain has supplied specimens of these translations which enable us to form some judgment of their value; since he distinguishes those made directly from the Greek text from those made from Arabic versions. The latter are not so inferior to the former as might have been expected; probably because the Arab scholars of the tenth and eleventh centuries knew more Greek than the European scholars of the twelfth and thirteenth; although sometimes the Arabic translation was made from an intermediate Syriac version.'—*Op. Maj.*, vol. i, p. 68 *n.*]

Dinant and Amaury of Bena. Though we know little of either, except through the criticism of their opponents, notably through that of Albert and Aquinas, yet such criticism is too detailed and definite to admit of doubt that their deductions from Aristotle and from his Arabian commentators led them to the assertion of the unity of substance; in other words, to the ultimate identity of matter, mind, and God. As quoted by Albert, the language of David was: 'It is manifest that there is one sole substance, not only of all bodies, but also of all souls, and that this is nothing but God Himself. God, matter, and mind are one and the same sole substance' (Albert, *Summa Theol.*, Pars II, tract. xii, quaest. 72, memb. 4, art. 2). David kept himself within the limits of philosophic theory. He is said to have been personally intimate with Innocent III; and at least during his lifetime his heresies escaped notice. It was otherwise with his contemporary Amaury of Bena, who, maintaining the same opinions, was condemned by the Pope and forced publicly to disavow them. But they survived in his disciples, who used them in ways directly hostile to Catholic faith and discipline. A council was held in Paris in 1209. Amaury's body was disinterred and buried in unconsecrated ground; several of his followers were burnt. It was at this council, the decrees of which were confirmed and enforced six years afterwards by Robert de Courçon, the Papal legate, that the study of the *Physics* and *Metaphysics* of Aristotle was prohibited, on the mistaken supposition that the ultimate source of these heresies was to be found there; a mistake due probably to the comments of Averroes, with which the first translations of these works into Latin were accompanied.[1]

How to deal with the problem of matter so as to give no countenance to pantheistic error was therefore an urgent and momentous question, to which the schoolmen of the thirteenth century, and Albert especially, devoted their full powers. Terrestrial substance, said Aristotle, was made up of matter and form. Apart from form, what then was matter? A pure essence, having the capacity, *potentia*, to become the subject of form, was the reply. How, then, distinguish matter from this *potentia*? Yet, if this be so, if matter is potentially the subject of all possible forms, we have in matter something that underlies all substance. Suppose all forms destroyed, matter

---

[1] See Jean de Launoy's work *De varia Aristotelis in Academia Parisiensi fortuna liber* (Paris, 1653), in which seven stages are noted, from the condemnation of Aristotle in 1209 to the condemnation of his opponents by the Parlement of Paris in 1624. *Cf.* Hauréau, *Hist. de la Philos. Scolast.*, Part II, vol. ii, pp. 75-119.

holding in itself all the conditions of existence still remains. How, then, distinguish matter from God?

Albert's attempted solution of the problem is involved and obscure in the extreme, and it must not occupy us here. We are concerned with Bacon's. Bacon attacked the problem in his own way, and with a full sense of its importance. His conclusions are expressed in the eighth chapter of the fourth part of the *Opus Majus*, and in the thirty-eighth chapter of the *Opus Tertium*; and a still further exposition of them is found in the unpublished[1] work of Bacon already mentioned, entitled *Communia Naturalium*. This treatise on Natural Philosophy consists of four parts, of which the discussion of Matter occupies the second.

Substance, Bacon maintains, can be predicated neither of matter nor of form; but only of the compound which results from their union. 'Compositum habet rationem per se existendi in ordine entium: non sic materia et forma.' Matter and form are not substances: substance results from their union. Proceeding from above downwards through the hierarchy of being in the order of increasing speciality, we have, as the genus generalissimum, 'Substantia composita universalis.' This may be corporeal or spiritual. Corporeal

[1] [See footnote on p. 42.]

substance may be terrestrial or celestial. Terrestrial substance may be a mixture of elements, or a single element. Mixed substance may be animate or inanimate. Animate substance may be sensitive (*i.e.* animal) or vegetal. Animal substance may be rational or irrational.

To each of these grades in the hierarchy of substance belong corresponding grades, not merely in the hierarchy of form, but also in the hierarchy of matter. 'Matter,' says Bacon, 'is not what most teachers of philosophy maintain it to be, unam numero.' In the descending scale from general to special, each grade of matter, like each grade of form, is distinct from the preceding. One kind of matter is separated from another by specific differences, just as form is separated from form. 'The difference between an ass and a horse is not a difference of form only; it is a difference of matter' (*Commun. Natur.*, Pars II, Dist. ii, cap. 6).

Bacon has condensed these views in the diagrammatic form shown in the subjoined schedules,[1] which I have copied from the Mazarine MS., pp. 23, 24. (They have been collated with those of the Br. Mus. MS. Royal 7 F. vii, fol.

---

[1] [These schedules have been omitted from this edition; they will be found in vol. i of the *Opus Majus*, also on pp. 87–9 of Mr Steele's edition of the *Communium Naturalium*.]

91 and 92. The variants in this MS. for the schedules of *substantia composita* and *forma* are unimportant. Those of *materia* are omitted; this MS. being in other respects less perfect than that of the Mazarine library.)

How are we to estimate these speculations? It is obvious in the first place that they stand in marked opposition to, or at least in distinction from, theories current among Bacon's contemporaries. To judge rightly of them we must bear in mind that throughout the greater part of the thirteenth century questions were being agitated of even greater importance than the controversy between realism and nominalism. The pantheistic tendencies discernible in Averroes and other Arabian thinkers had been diffused, as we have seen, by men like Amaury and David of Dinant. They were responsible, as some thought, for the disastrous anarchy which early in the century had devastated southern France. Bacon was quick to perceive the danger of maintaining the unity of matter. It had been defended, as he points out (*Op. Maj.*, vol. i, p. 144), by passages from Aristotle which he wishes to believe had been badly translated. In any case, he says, 'the error is enormous, as great as any that can possibly be found in speculative questions. If it be granted, it is impossible to comprehend the generation of things, and the whole course of nature will be misunderstood. And what is more, if this error be looked at closely, it will be found to tend towards heresy, or rather to be the profanest of heresies, since the inevitable result of it is to endow matter with the creative power of God.' Whatever dangers were involved in the unity of matter, Bacon met by a bold denial of such unity. 'Divide et impera,' he said in effect; matter, thus split up into sections, is no longer to be feared.

Looking at Bacon's theory by the light of subsequent centuries, it is not difficult to see that its value lay in its solvent and destructive power. His aim from beginning to end of his career was to draw men away from verbal subtleties and concentrate them on the realities of life, as plain men understand them. 'You ask me,' he would say to the young students around him, 'what is this matter which remains apart from all form, with capacity for receiving all? But who told you that it was one and indivisible? There are as many kinds and degrees of matter as there are of things. Look at the things, try them, see how they act on you, how you can act on them. As to the matter and form that may underlie them, leave that to God.'

Bacon's part in the great controversy between

realism and nominalism will lead us to a similar conclusion. It was a less burning controversy in the thirteenth century than in the days of Roscellinus and Abelard, or than it became afterwards in the days of Duns Scotus and William of Ockham; and it was debated by Albert and by Aquinas with the far larger and deeper understanding of its complications, that might be expected from men who were not merely trained like their predecessors in the study of Aristotle's Logic, but had become conversant with the problems raised in his *Physics* and *Metaphysics*. Both these thinkers rejected the independent existence of universals *in re* as clearly as Aristotle had done. They were clear that universals had no existence except in the mind. 'Non est universale nisi dum intelligitur' (Albert, *Met.*, lib. v, tract. vi, cap. 7). 'Una et eadem natura quae singularis erat et individuatur per materiam in singularibus hominibus efficitur postea universalis per actionem intellectus depurantis illam a conditionibus quae sunt hic et nunc' (Aquinas, *Tractatus primus de universalibus*). Nevertheless, both of them left a place for the universal *ante rem*, not indeed in the fantastic world of Ideas which Plato had portrayed, but as radiations centred in the primal form, the mind of God.

Turning to Bacon, who discusses the question

of universals at considerable length and with extreme independence, we find the same tendency to emancipate himself from bondage to words, entities, and verbal discussions, and to dig down to a foundation of solid fact. One individual, he says,[1] is of more account than all the universals in the world. A universal is nothing but the similarity of several individuals; 'convenientia plurium individuorum.' 'Two things,' he goes on to say, 'are needful for the individual. The first is absolute: it is that which constitutes his existence, as when we say, "This man is made of soul and body." The second is that in which he resembles another man, and not an ass or a pig. This is his universal. But the absolute nature of an individual is of far more importance than his related nature. It is fixed and absolute by itself. Thus the singular is of more account (*nobilius*) than its universal. Experience leads us to this conclusion, ... and so also does theology. God has not created the world for the sake of the universal man, but for the sake of individual persons.' 'Individuum est natura absoluta et fixa habens esse per se; et universale non est nisi convenientia individui respectu alterius.'

---

[1] On the question of universals, and also on that of individuation, *cf.* the extracts from the *Communia Naturalium* given by Émile Charles, pp. 383–6.

In some passages Bacon appears to go much further in the direction of nominalism than Albert and Aquinas. 'The prevalent view,' he remarks, 'is that universals exist only in the mind. Yet two stones would be like one another, even though there should be no mind to perceive them. But it is precisely this likeness of the two stones that constitutes their universal' (*Commun. Natur.*, Pars II, Dist. ii, cap. 10).

Closely allied with the controversy as to universals was the question of individuation. Are things individualized by form or by matter? Albert and Aquinas took the latter view, Bonaventura the former. 'Individuorum multitudo,' says Albert (*De Coelo*, tract. iii, cap. 8), 'fit omnis per divisionem materiae. Formae quae sunt receptibiles in materia individuantur per materiam.' (*Cf.* Aquinas, *Summa Theol.*, Pars I, quaest. iii, art. 2.) Aquinas was obliged, however, to add that this 'materia' must be 'signata': must be quantified. 'Signatio ejus est esse sub certis signationibus quae faciunt esse hic et nunc.' This addition went far to neutralize the Thomist view of individuation; for as his opponents at once rejoined, 'What determines quantity if not form?'

In opposition to Aquinas, Bonaventura maintained that 'species est totum esse individui.' Substance consisting of the union of matter and form, matter was uniform in all : the form was that which distinguished or individualized.

Bacon (*Commun. Natur.*, Pars II, Dist. ii, cap. 9), in opposition to either view, maintained that the question was meaningless and foolish. All substances, whether universal or singular, have their own constitutive principles. Soul and body make man. This soul and this body make this man. In the intention and procedure of nature, 'this man' is prior to 'man'; 'man' comes in as something subsidiary, 'extra essentiam ejus, similem accidenti,' as the means of comparison with other individuals. There is no more reason for inquiring what causes individuation than for inquiring what causes universality. There is no answer to such a question, except that the Creator makes everything as its nature requires. Individual matter and form is made in one way: specific or generic matter and form is made in another. 'Stultitia magna est in hujusmodi quaestione quam faciunt de individuatione.'

III. BACON'S *SCRIPTUM PRINCIPALE*[1]

The foregoing remarks, which it would be easy, but not, in this place, justifiable to prolong,

---

[1] [In his excellent bibliographical appendix to Dr Rashdall's ed. of the *Compendium Studii Theologiae* (1911), Mr Little calls

SCRIPTUM PRINCIPALE

will illustrate Bacon's position as a schoolman, thoroughly versed in the technique of scholastic controversy. But he was a schoolman whom a long and laborious study of the realities of life, whether in nature or in man, had taught to distinguish things from words : solid facts from subtle figments. He was not alone in this. Albert and Aquinas were solid thinkers like himself. Less versed in natural science than Bacon, they had more than he to do with the science of man ; they had to face the difficult and urgent problems connected with the spiritual government of mankind. Their philosophy, like his, dealt with real things. And if theirs was less positive, less free from metaphysical figments, it is only that the complications of human nature were less adapted for positive treatment than the physical phenomena to which Bacon devoted so large a share of his attention.

But in contrast with these three great schoolmen stand the weavers of word-systems, like Alexander of Hales, Henry of Ghent, and Duns Scotus, wasting their own and other men's time and energy in defining, dividing, and refining with infinite

this projected work of Bacon the *Compendium Philosophiae*. The title *Magnum Opus* is adopted by Mr Steele in his ed. of the *Metaphysica*. The terms *Scriptum Principale* and *Compendium Philosophiae* were both used by Bacon to denote this work.]

ingenuity, and with such result as when children build sand-castles on the shore. With such men it may have been needful to fight, yet fighting was but beating the air. Of what avail to discuss individuation with dialecticians who explained it by '*haecceitas*[1]'?

In all Bacon's discussion of scholastic problems, the solution he reached was of a kind to favour the falling off of the metaphysical husk, and to bring to light the real and positive problem which lay beneath it. His scholastic theories are therefore for us, and in all probability were for him, of far greater negative than constructive value. But his central aim lay in another direction above and beyond scholasticism. We shall best learn how to appreciate it by looking at the programme of the

---

[1] This word is believed to be due rather to the disciples of Duns Scotus than to the master himself. Happily for Bacon's peace of mind, he did not live to witness the triumphal career of the Doctor Subtilis. Of Hauréau's careful appreciation of his work the final words may be quoted: 'Cette philosophie n'explique pas la nature, elle l'invente; substituant l'ordre rationnel à l'ordre réel, elle dispense, il est vrai, de l'étude des choses; mais, quand après avoir admiré l'économie d'un système si complet, si habilement ordonné, on abaisse ses regards vers ces choses dont on a jusqu'alors dédaigné de s'enquérir, on soupçonne dès l'abord qu'on vient d'achever un rêve, et bientôt, devant le spectacle qu'offre la réalité, s'effacent, s'évanouissent l'une après l'autre toutes les abstractions décevantes, toutes les chimères dont la création appartient au système, à lui seul.'—*Hist. de la Philos. Scolast.*, Part II, vol. ii, pp. 171-259, ed. 1872-80.

SCRIPTUM PRINCIPALE 57

encyclopædic work, the *Scriptum Principale*, often spoken of in the *Opus Majus* and the *Opus Tertium*, but of which the persecutions and imprisonment of his later life never allowed him to execute more than a few fragments. And of these fragments many are lost.

This *Scriptum Principale*, as he tells us in the first chapter of the unpublished[1] work entitled *Communia Naturalium*, consisted, or was intended to consist, of four volumes. The first volume dealt with Grammar and Logic, the second with Mathematics, the third with the Natural Sciences, the fourth with Metaphysics and Morals.

The second chapter of the *Communia Naturalium* is entitled, 'De numero et ordine scientiarum naturalium.' He distinguishes eight natural sciences. The first treats of the principles common to Natural Philosophy. The others are :—(1) Perspective or Optics,[2] (2) Astronomy,[3] (3) Barology, (4) Alchemy, (5) Agriculture, (6) Medicine, (7) Experimental Science. The general principles of Natural Science form the subject of

[1] [See footnote on p. 42.]

[2] [The Optics of the *Scriptum Principale* may probably be regarded as represented by the *De Mult. Spec.*, which undoubtedly formed part of the former work.]

[3] [The astronomical section of the projected third volume of the *Scriptum Principale* has been published as follows :—*Liber Secundus Commun. Natur. F. R. De Celestibus.* Ed. R. Steele. Clarendon Press, Oxford, 1913.]

the first treatise here spoken of.¹ Of the seven special sciences, the first three form part of what would in the present day be called Physics. Under Astronomy is included not merely the study of planetary motions, but the scientific determination of terrestrial positions, in other words, Geography, and also the influence of the stars and the sun on the earth and man: that is to say, the study of climate and of astrological forces. As to the third of the special sciences, 'scientia de elementis,' or as he also calls it, 'scientia de Ponderibus,' what in the present day would be called Barology, it is not without interest to find it thus set apart as a distinct department of speculation. The fourth, Alkimia, corresponds, so far as the description of its purpose goes, very nearly to the modern science of Chemistry. It deals, says Bacon, with the 'mixtiones elementorum,' with the generation of liquids, gases, and solids ('humores et spiritus et corpora'), with all inanimate substances, including organic products ('usque ad partes animalium et plantarum inclusive').

The title of the fifth science, Agricultura, would be misleading, if Bacon had not given us a clear explanation of its purpose.² It is the science of

¹ [*i.e.* the *Communia Naturalium.*]
² *Cf.* the long extract given by Charles, pp. 370-4. The unfortunate rarity of Charles's work is my excuse for citing the portion of this extract relating to the study of living bodies,

living bodies, vegetal and animal; reserving, however, the subject of man's physical nature for subsequent treatment under the head of medicine. Before man can be properly investigated, we must know the nature and surroundings of other animate things. First we must distinguish the soil fit for different kinds of plants, arable land, forest land, pasture land, garden land. We then examine the whole subject of plants which has been left incomplete in the treatise attributed to Aristotle, *De Vegetabilibus*. But as lands cannot be tilled without domestic animals, and as forests, pastures, and deserts depend for their value on the wild animals they contain, the science we are now speaking of embraces the full consideration of animal life on which, as Bacon believed, Aristotle wrote far more volumes than have come down to us. In the sixth science [Medicine] we proceed to the study of the animal possessing reason, the study of Man. Our aim being to understand the conditions of his health or disease, we have first to examine his structure and development, with-

based, as Bacon explains, on the preliminary study of *Alkimia Speculativa*. [The Latin quotation from Charles's work, of which Dr Bridges gives a summary in the remainder of the paragraph, has been omitted from this edition. It will be found on pp. 7–9 of Mr Steele's edition of the *Communium Naturalium*: 'Deinceps de plantarum natura et animalium . . . erit inter naturales comprehensa.']

out which health and disease cannot be understood or spoken of.

Finally, to complete the whole, comes Experimental Science. It is, he says, a final judge of the assertions and reasonings put forth in all the foregoing sciences. More than this: it gives directions to those engaged in other sciences as to the construction of instruments by which their conclusions are to be tested, in the same way in which a navigator instructs a shipwright as to the building of a ship. Thus, for instance, it instructs the geometer to make a mirror such that the rays reflected from it shall converge in a single point. It scrutinizes every natural, every artificial force. It sifts the artifices of magic, as logic sifts the reasonings of the sophist, so as to dissipate falsehood and error, and leave nothing but truth remaining.

How Bacon would have treated this part of the subject we have no means of judging, other than the sixth section of the *Opus Majus*. But even the summary exposition there given is enough to show how large was his conception of experimental method, and at the same time how carefully he steered clear of the danger of undervaluing the mathematical or deductive process of discovery. So far as was possible the two should be pursued simultaneously and in close alliance. Euclid's

SCRIPTUM PRINCIPALE

demonstration of his first proposition would, he says, fail to carry complete conviction unless visual evidence of it were forthcoming in the construction of the figure. And on the other hand, we see that his inductive investigations of the rainbow were controlled at every step by deductions from astronomy.[1]

With these general remarks, we may now pass to each of the principal divisions of the *Scriptum Principale*, which in the main correspond to the order followed in the *Opus Majus*.[2] First comes Language [Grammar and Logic], as the channel through which the thoughts of other men are handed down to us; then follows Mathematics, embracing the four branches of the Quadrivium, geometry, arithmetic, astronomy, and music. Thence we pass to Natural Science, which included the study of the propagation of force, specially illustrated by the radiation of light and heat. Next comes Alkimia Speculativa, not the mere metallurgy of the gold-seekers, but the study of the transformation of matter from its simplest to its most complicated state. The study of living matter [Agriculture] followed, ending with Medicine, the science dealing with the physical

[1] [See Note F (*b*) on p. 158.]
[2] [See Note C (Table of the Seven Parts of the *Opus Majus*), and Note D (Table of the *Scriptum Principale*), on pp. 151, 152.]

structure of man. Finally, the edifice of the sciences is crowned by Ethics and Metaphysics.

Of this comprehensive scheme let us see what fragments are forthcoming.

IV. BACON'S PHILOLOGY

In urging that the comparative study of language should form part of the University curriculum, Bacon stood nearly alone. He does indeed full justice to those among his contemporaries who had promoted the translation of Greek books into Latin ; and, first among those, to the illustrious Bishop of Lincoln, his forerunner and counsellor. But though Grosseteste had caused many books to be translated for the sake of their contents, it does not appear that he or anyone else had proposed to carry the study of language, as such, beyond the routine of grammar presented in the Trivium ; the Latin accidence and syntax of Priscian or Donatus.

What Bacon proposed was the systematic and comparative study of Hebrew, Arabic, and Greek, with the dialects belonging to each. With Hebrew went Chaldæan, and, in more distant relationship, Arabic : with Greek its various dialects, which were, he tells us, comparable to the Picard,

PHILOLOGY 63

Norman, or Burgundian dialects of French, or to the northern, southern, eastern, and western dialects of English. 'I do not mean,' says Bacon, 'that every one should learn these languages as he learns his mother tongue, so as to be able to speak them as we speak English, French, and Latin; nor again that we should content ourselves with being able to translate into our own language the Latin versions. There is an intermediate degree of attainment quite easy to those who have teachers. We should know enough to be able to understand how these languages should be rendered in Latin. The point is that a man should be able to read these languages, and understand their grammatical structure' ('accidentia partium orationis,' *Comp. Stud. Phil.*, ed. Brewer, p. 434).

What Bacon's linguistic attainments were cannot be precisely decided. No work of his, published or unpublished, that I am aware of, affords evidence of knowledge of Arabic. His own words in the twenty-fifth chapter of the *Opus Tertium* are scarcely decisive on the point. 'De Arabica tango locis suis; sed nihil scribo Arabice, sicut Hebraee, Graece, et Latine, quia evidentius et facilius ostenditur propositum meum in his. Nam pro studio theologiae parum valet, licet pro philosophia multum, et pro conversione infidelium.' Some pages printed for the first time in this edition show acquaintance at least with the Hebrew alphabet. An elementary Greek grammar, in the possession of Corpus Christi College, Oxford, testifies to his knowledge of Greek, which indeed is sufficiently apparent in the present work, and still more in the ninth and following chapters of the *Compendium Studii Philosophiae* (Brewer, pp. 495–519). This grammar is incomplete, dealing chiefly with the alphabet, with the Greek system of accentuation, aspiration, and quantity, and with the numeral system. It concludes with the paradigm of the verb τύπτω. Its opening sentence seems to indicate that it formed a part of Bacon's encyclopædic work. 'Here begins the first book of the volume on the grammar of languages other than Latin. This book deals with Greek grammar.' 'I have already,' he continues, 'spoken of the advantage to the Latin world of knowing the four languages, Greek, Hebrew, Arabic, and Chaldæan; and in the preface to this volume devoted to grammar I have explained the division of subjects and their order. I now proceed to consider Greek grammar, beginning with such rudiments as boys are taught in Latin in order that they may read, write, and construe simple passages, and may pass thence to points of greater difficulty.'[1]

[1] [The existing portions of this grammar were published at

PHILOLOGY

A point of interest presents itself as to Bacon's pronunciation of Greek. Much attention is given to the transliteration of the Greek alphabet into its Latin equivalents. The Lord's Prayer, the Salutation to the Virgin, and the Apostles' Creed are written out in Latin, underlined first with the Greek words in Roman characters, and secondly with the same words in Greek. The second of these is here given as an example :

Ave Maria graciosa dominus cum tui benedicta
xere Maria kecharitomeni o kirios meta su eulogimeni
χαῖρε μαρία κεχάριτωμένη ὁ κυρίος μετὰ σοῦ ευλογήμένη

tu in mulieribus et benedictus fructus ventris tui
si en ginexi ke eulogimenos o karpos tis kilias su
σὺ ἐν γιναιξὶ καὶ ευλογίμενος ὁ καρπος τῆς κοιλίας σοῦ

amen.
amin.
'αμήν.

It is evident from the transliteration of vowels and diphthongs here adopted, with which may be compared pp. 75–6 of the *Opus Majus*, printed for the first time in this edition, that these were pronounced as in modern Greek.[1] It appears also in

the Cambridge Press in 1902 as follows : *The Greek Grammar of Roger Bacon and a Fragment of his Hebrew Grammar.* Ed. w. intr. and notes by E. Nolan and S. A. Hirsch.]

[1] In the Corpus Christi Coll. Grammar, a systematic scheme of transliteration and of pronunciation is also given. We learn

the subsequent discussion on accents, that accents were considered, no less than quantity, in pronunciation. Bacon may not improbably have learnt the language from one of the Greeks who had been invited into England by Grosseteste. Some of these, he tells us, had become permanent residents. (In *Comp. Stud. Phil.*, ed. Brewer, pp. 495–514, the same subject is treated.)

In urging so strongly the study of language, Bacon had two main purposes in view: an improved text of the Bible, and an intelligible translation of Aristotle.[1] Under both these heads the

from it that the second letter of the alphabet was pronounced like the modern English *v*; and that there was no single letter rendering the sound of our *b*. 'Item π post μ vel ν, sive in eadem dictione, sive in diversis, dummodo sine intervallo proferantur, sonum nostri *b* habet, quam aliter non habent, ut λαμπάς, ἄμπελον. Similiter τ post μ vel ν sonat nostrum *d*, quod aliter non habent, ut ἀντίχριστος.' All this is in accordance with modern Greek pronunciation. The transliteration of the diphthongs αυ and ευ was a matter of some difficulty owing to the confusion between *u* and *v*. Bacon usually renders them as *af* and *ef*. But in modern Greek it is only before θ, κ, ξ, π, σ, τ, φ, χ, ψ, that they are thus pronounced; before other letters they would have the sound of *av* or *ev*. With regard to accents, Bacon's language (both in the Corpus Christi MS. and in the *Comp. Stud. Phil.*) puts it beyond all doubt that they governed his pronunciation of the language.

[1] ['It was not merely for the sake of Biblical and philosophic culture that Bacon advocated the study of language. It was needed for our commerce in the Mediterranean, where the want of it involved our traders in heavy losses. It was needed still more for foreign missions, and for papal diplomacy with the

PHILOLOGY 67

minor works, edited by Brewer, contain much for which in the *Opus Majus* Bacon had not found room. With regard to the first, the valuable memoir published in 1888 by Abbé Martin may be consulted.[1] It appears that, towards the end of the twelfth or the beginning of the thirteenth century, a text of the Bible had become generally current in Paris under the title of ' Textus Parisiensis.' Bacon, writing in 1267, speaks of it as having been hastily compiled, about forty years before, by second-rate theologians and carelessly copied by uncritical booksellers (*Op. Min.*, ed. Brewer, p. 333). It abounded in errors and in interpolations inserted from patristic quotations, from liturgies, and from the works of Josephus. Many of these errors attracted notice, and attempts were made, principally by members of the mendicant Orders, to correct them. But these attempts, in Bacon's judgment, only resulted in making the matter worse. Each critic worked independently and without adequate critical apparatus. Not merely did Franciscan differ from Dominican, but the members of each Order

East. When the Sultan of Babylon sent a letter in Arabic to Saint Louis, not a single man, he tells us, could be found in the University of Paris to decipher or answer the letter.'—*E. and A.*, p. 183.]

[1] [*La Vulgate Latine au xiiie siècle d'après Roger Bacon.* Paris, 1888.]

differed amongst themselves. Successive corrected versions were put forward, each worse than the preceding. By the middle of the century the Paris text had fallen into hopeless confusion; and it had become, in Bacon's judgment, far the lesser evil to use the uncorrected text than any of those which had been so uncritically amended. Of these strong remarks he gives many pointed illustrations.

So devoid were these successive editors, not merely of linguistic knowledge, but of the critical spirit, that they seem to have been entirely unaware of the origin and history of the Vulgate. Bacon's history of the various Biblical versions, ending with that of Jerome, as given in the *Opus Minus*, pp. 334–349, is not one of the least interesting portions of his work. His principal result was to show that, before Jerome's translation from the Hebrew, the version regarded as authentic by the Church was the Septuagint; although theologians had felt themselves at liberty to correct that version from that of Aquila, Symmachus, and above all of Theodotion. After the time of Jerome, the translation from the Septuagint continued to be used in the Psalter; but, with that exception, Jerome's translation from the Hebrew constituted the Vulgate, and was received as authentic by the Church. Bacon is careful to add

PHILOLOGY 69

that Jerome's version is by no means free from error, due partly to over-haste, partly to his unwillingness to offend his contemporaries by making too many changes in the text hitherto accepted.

With Aristotle the case was even worse than with the Bible. The brilliant hopes with which the century had opened, of re-entering the temple of Greek wisdom, and listening to the voice of the greatest of ancient thinkers, had been falsified by the failure of Aristotle's translators to comply with the two elementary conditions of translation; knowledge of the language in which, and comprehension of the subject about which, the book was written. Something has already been said (p. 43) of the Toledo school of translators instituted by Archbishop Raymond in the twelfth century. A new and vigorous impulse was given forty or fifty years afterwards by the Emperor Frederic II, whose preference of Mohammedanism to Christianity, had he occupied a humbler station, would assuredly have subjected him to a worse fate than that of Bacon. Leaving out of account translations of Aristotle's *Organon*, parts of which were familiar to the western world from the times of Augustine and Boethius,[1] the translators of Aristotle's

---

[1] ['Boethius is stated in a letter written to him by Theodoric, preserved in Cassiodorus, to have translated many Greek scientific works, notably those of Euclid, Archimedes, and

philosophic and scientific work in the twelfth and thirteenth century, to whom Bacon calls attention, were five : Gerard of Cremona, Alured of England, Michael Scot, Hermann the German, William of Moerbeke, otherwise called the Fleming. Of these, Gerard, Scot, and Hermann translated from Arabic versions. Gerard spent many years in Spain, attained a thorough knowledge of Arabic, and translated Ptolemy's *Almagest*, and Aristotle's *Meteorologica*, also the astronomy of Alfraganus, several works of Al-Kindi, and, almost certainly, the *Optics* of Alhazen. He died in 1187. Michael Scot flourished in the first half of the thirteenth century. He was a friend of the Emperor Frederic II, under whose patronage he visited Spain, and translated from the Arabic many of Aristotle's works, with the comments of Averroes. Albertus Magnus says of him that he was ignorant of natural things, and that he did not thoroughly understand Aristotle's books. Bacon, who speaks of the impression produced in the schools when he appeared in 1230,[1] with translations of Aristotle's

Ptolemy. Among the authors mentioned in this letter is Aristoteles *logicus*. Of Aristotle's *Physics* and *Metaphysics* there is no mention ; and certainly nothing was known of Aristotle in Christian Europe during the eleventh and twelfth centuries, except the 'aliqua logicalia' of which Bacon speaks.'— *Op. Maj.*, vol. iii, p. 161.]

[1] ['In 1230, Bacon tells us, in the thirteenth chapter of the

metaphysical and scientific treatises, says that he was ignorant of words and of things, and that the greater part of his work was due to Andrew the Jew.[1] Scot's translation of Avicenna's treatise *De Animalibus*, as I have remarked in a note (vol. ii, p. 85),[2] certainly seems to bear out this severe judgment. Hermann the German was

second part of the *Opus Majus*, " Michael Scot appeared on the scene, bringing with him certain portions of Aristotle's works on Natural Science and Metaphysics, with authentic comments. From this time the philosophy of Aristotle has been magnified throughout the Western world (*inter Latinos*)." . . . Scot's advent in Oxford was for Roger Bacon the startling event which turned his attention to the study of the scientific writings of Aristotle and his successors in the Greek and in the Arabian world.'—*E. and A.*, p. 167.]

[1] [Although Bacon had a poor opinion of Scot's abilities, derived from Hermann, Dr Bridges was mistaken in supposing that Bacon ever said that Scot was 'ignorant of words and of things, and that the greater part of his work was due to Andrew the Jew.' The words just quoted are a translation of Jebb's own Latin in his preface to the *Op. Maj.* of 1733. Mr J. Wood Brown fell into the same mistake in his biography of Scot (1897), as is pointed out on p. liii of *The Greek Grammar of R. B.* (1902).]

[2] ['This work, translated by Michael Scotus, and dedicated to his patron the Emperor Frederic II, was printed in Venice in 1500. The book is not so distinctly a commentary on Aristotle as are the principal philosophical works of Averroes and Aquinas, though it follows to some extent the Aristotelian arrangement. Not knowing Arabic, I cannot speak of the accuracy of the translation. But it is clumsily and ungrammatically written, is filled with untranslated Arabic words, and gives the impression that the translator knew little of the subject.'— *Op. Maj.*, vol. ii, p. 85 *n.*]

personally known to Bacon; he worked in Spain, and, with the help of Arab interpreters, produced translations of the *Rhetoric*, *Poetics*, and *Ethics* of Aristotle. He mentions incidentally (Jourdain, p. 140) that Grosseteste had produced a more complete rendering of the *Ethics* directly from the Greek. Hermann, in answer to some questions put to him by Bacon as to Aristotle's logical works, frankly confessed his ignorance of logic. 'Nor was he well acquainted,' Bacon continues, 'with Arabic, being rather an encourager of translations than a translator himself; the principal part of his work was done by Saracens in his employment' (*Comp. Stud. Phil.*, cap. 8).

William the Fleming (of Moerbeke) had the advantage over these men that he translated directly from the Greek. His work is believed to have been done at the special request of Thomas Aquinas, who made use of it in his Commentaries on Aristotle. 'But it was notorious in Paris,' says Bacon, 'that William of Moerbeke was totally ignorant of science, and his translations are consequently full of errors.' On the whole, he concludes that it would have been better that Aristotle should never have been translated, rather than that such a mass of error should be propagated under the shelter of his name. 'Had I the power of disposing of these works, I would have them all burnt: it is a waste of time to study them, a source of error and of diffusion of ignorance greater than can be described.' 'Aristotle's works,' he continues, 'are the foundation of all wisdom, but they must be studied in the original to be of any profit' (*Comp. Stud. Phil.*, ed. Brewer, p. 469).

Everyone who considers Bacon's efforts in promoting the study of language must agree with Professor Brewer (p. lxii) that 'his labours in this respect have attracted less attention than they deserve. . . . It is as creditable to his discernment as to his courage that he should have seen, better than Lord Bacon did, the paramount importance of philology, and urged it repeatedly on his contemporaries. It is amazing to hear a scholar of the thirteenth century insisting on the necessity of constant references to original authorities as the only sure foundation of sacred criticism.'

It may be that Bacon's exhortations, reiterated, as we feel sure they would be, not in writing merely, but in conversation with the young men whom he gathered round him, were not entirely without effect on the following generation. In the council convoked in 1312 by Clement V at Vienne, one of the provisions, says Fleury (*Hist. Eccl.*, liv. 91), was 'the establishment in the Roman

Curia, and in the Universities of Paris, Oxford, Bologna, and Salamanca, of teachers for the three languages, Hebrew, Arabic, and Chaldæan, two for each. They were to be maintained in Rome by the Pope, in Paris by the King of France, and in the other cities by the prelates, bishops, and chapters of the country.' This subject has been carefully studied by Mr Rashdall in his important work on the Universities of Europe in the Middle Ages. He gives strong authority for the belief that Greek was included; and if so, the avowed purpose of the ordinance, which was the conversion of the Mohammedans and Jews, may not have been the only purpose; some faint echo of Bacon's exhortation to study Aristotle and the Bible in the original, with the view of understanding them better, may have been still audible. Few and short-lived were the attempts made to carry the decree of this council into effect. In 1320 we hear of a rate levied upon benefices in the province of Canterbury for the support of a converted Jew alleged to be teaching Greek at Oxford. But Oxford was already passing under the spell of the enchanter. The fine webs of Duns Scotus, which the sword of Ockham might cleave but could not dissipate, were paralyzing her energies. Five generations were to pass before she could again begin to promote the study

MATHEMATICS

of 'languages other than Latin'[1]; and even then not in the comprehensive spirit which Bacon had advocated. It is tempting, though painful and perhaps useless, to imagine how far European culture might have advanced had schools of Oriental languages, concurrently with those of Greek and Latin, been instituted and continuously maintained from the thirteenth century.

V. BACON'S MATHEMATICS

In the *Opus Majus*,[2] though much is said of the importance and necessity of mathematical method, there is very little display of mathematical knowledge. Frequent references are made to Euclid, whose *Elements* had been introduced to the western world early in the previous century, by Adelard of Bath, and more completely in the thirteenth century by Campanus of Novara. Archimedes and Apollonius are rarely mentioned. But in his *Optics* Bacon shows that he was acquainted with the properties of parabolic con-

[1] The organized teaching of Greek in Oxford is due to Richard Fox, the founder of Corpus Christi College (1515-16). But when Erasmus was in Oxford about twenty years earlier, such men as Thomas Linacre and William Grocyn had already become Greek scholars, under the teaching, perhaps, of Cornelio Vitelli. (*Cf.* Hallam, *Lit. Hist. of Europe*, part i, ch. 3.)

[2] [Part IV.]

cave mirrors, and of their power of causing parallel rays to converge after reflexion to a focus. In this respect he was in advance of his principal teachers in Optics, Euclid, Ptolemy, and Alhazen.

Of the Calculus, arithmetical or algebraical, Bacon has but slight occasion to speak in the *Opus Majus*. It has always to be remembered that this work, with its appendices, the *Opus Minus* and *Opus Tertium*, was not, properly speaking, a philosophical treatise, but an exhortation addressed to a statesman, absorbed in ecclesiastical and political struggles, to exert his authority for the revival of learning. Hence it is uniformly spoken of as a *Persuasio*. It contains just as much learning and science as was thought needful to convince the Pope that learning and science were capable of strengthening the Church. It is but the preamble to the *Scriptum Principale*, which there is reason for thinking that Bacon had already begun, but which he regretfully expresses his inability to send at such short notice. Hence though it deals, often very cursorily, with every department of knowledge then recognized, we must not infer Bacon's ignorance of a subject from the fact that this provisional treatise makes no mention of it.

Among the fragments of the *Scriptum Principale*

MATHEMATICS

which have come down to us is a portion of the first book on Mathematics,[1] preserved among the Sloane MSS. (2156). This first book contained three parts. We have the first part of this book, and a considerable part of the second. A few fragments more are to be found in the Bodleian (Digby MSS. 76). As far as I am aware, nothing more is extant.

The first part deals with preliminary principles ('quaedam communia praeambula ad interiora mathematicae').

It has five divisions or distinctions. The subjects dealt with [in the first] are the relation of mathematics to metaphysics; its distinction from magic; the hindrances to its culture offered by the four causes of error, namely, false conceit of wisdom, authority, custom, and popular prejudice; the utility of mathematics, its importance to the preliminary studies of logic and grammar. The final chapter of this section is curious. The final purpose, says Bacon, of logic is conviction. But conviction is not reached by argumentative process alone, but by the arts of rhetoric and poetry, which are therefore in a true sense departments of logic. But these arts are governed by the laws of music, which is a branch of mathematical science.

[1] [*Communia Mathematicae.*]

The second division deals with the definition of the parts of quantity. Certain general terms, such as simultaneity in space and time, limit, continuity, infinity, dimension, are explained. The distinction is drawn between continuous and discrete quantity. Continuous quantity in one, two, and three dimensions is defined. Discrete quantity is distinguished into what is permanent, as number ; what is not permanent, as sound.

The third division expounds the distinction between the speculative and the practical departments of geometry and of arithmetic. The section on practical or applied geometry is of much interest as illustrating Bacon's enlarged views of scientific training. He indicates eight departments of this branch of science. (1) Agriculture,[1] in a far wider sense than is usually given to the word, comprising mensuration, architecture, civil, mechanical, and military engineering. (2) The fabrication of astronomical instruments. (3) Of musical instruments. (4) Of optical instruments. (5) Of barological instruments. (6) Of instruments of experimental science. (7) Of

[1] [Bacon uses this word in two different senses, to be carefully distinguished. In the *Communia Naturalium* he means by 'Agricultura' the study of soils, plants, and animals. But in the *Communia Mathematicae* he denotes by this word not only what we usually term 'Agriculture,' but several studies involving the use of practical geometry.]

MATHEMATICS 79

medical and surgical appliances. (8) Of chemical apparatus.

In connexion with the practical branch of arithmetic, after speaking of the use of the Abacus, he mentions 'vias algorithmi, scilicet quomodo conjugantur numeri et dividuntur, secundum omnem speciem algorithmi, tam in particularibus fractionibus quam in integris.' In this connexion he speaks of 'Algebra quae est negotiatio, et almochabala quae est census.' How far Bacon had assimilated the work of Mohammed ben Musa,[1] whose surname, Al-Khwarizmi, is incorporated in the word *Algorithm*, we cannot tell. But with the work of one of the two great mathematicians of the thirteenth century, Jordanus Nemorarius, he was certainly familiar, as may be seen by reference to vol. i, pp. 158, 169 of the

[1] Mohammed ben Musa Al-Khwarizmi was born in the first quarter of the ninth century. He constructed astronomical tables for the Caliph Al-Mamun, which were translated into Latin by Adelard of Bath. Of more importance, however, are his Arithmetic and his Algebra. The first of these remained for a long time unknown. But it was discovered in Cambridge in 1857, and is included among the *Trattati d' Aritmetica* published by Boncompagni. A full account of this work and of the Algebra, translated and edited by Rosen (London, 1831), will be found in Cantor, vol. i, pp. 611-29. Cantor (p. 612) explains clearly the passage of the word *Al-Khwarizmi* into *Algorithm*. Bacon's interpretation of the words 'Aldschebr walmuḳâbala,' which Al-Khwarizmi uses, is incorrect. Dschebr means restoration, muḳâbala means opposition.

Opus Majus. Among other branches of practical arithmetic he includes the construction of astronomical tables, mensuration, alloys and coinage, partnership, and other operations of commerce. These things are treated of at great length in the *Liber Abaci* of Leonardo of Pisa, the other great mathematician of the time, whose work, dedicated to Michael Scot, Bacon had possibly seen and studied; though he makes no mention of it, in any work known to us.[1]

Astrology and astronomy come next. The first is the speculative branch, dealing with planetary motions, with the figure of the earth and of its various regions.[2] Astronomy, the practical branch, has to do with the construction of tables and with the forecast of future events. Bacon admits that this use of the words has not been universally adopted, but maintains its correctness. 'Astrologia componitur ex hoc nomine astron, quod est stella, et hoc nomine logos, quod est verbum vel ratio vel sermo, quia est sermo de stellis. Astronomia vero dicitur lex stellarum, et nomos est lex. Unde quia lex universaliter sonat in practicam, ut in morali philosophia lex est ipsa

---

[1] To each of these two mathematicians Cantor devotes a full chapter. Cf. *Gesch. der Math.*, vol. ii, pp. 3–79.

[2] [For an account of the geographical section of Part IV of the *Opus Majus*, see Note E on p. 153.]

practica, ita similiter Astronomia est practica Astrologiae.'

In the fourth division music is considered. This includes not merely sound but gesture. Audible music is considered under the two heads of vocal and instrumental. In the vocal division every branch of elocution is included. Finally, the effect of music on the temper and health both of men and of animals should be systematically studied.

Abstraction is the subject of the fifth division. First we have the abstraction common to all science, since science deals with universals, not with particulars. There is then the abstraction of a first cause from secondary causes and of spirit from body, which the metaphysician deals with. Mathematical abstraction has to do with the study of quantity apart from the substance to which it belongs : apart from all natural changes such as growth, diminution, or change of place.

This first part closes with an explanation of the difference between axioms, postulates, and definitions.

The second part begins with the study of whole numbers and fractions : passing from this to the subject of arithmetical, geometrical, and harmonic ratio, and to the question of proportion generally. Continuous and discontinuous proportion are considered; and Euclid's definition of proportion is carefully considered.

Here the portion of the work contained in the Sloane MSS. ends. We find it continued, however, in a somewhat fragmentary way in the Bodleian Digby MSS. No. 76. The author proceeds to the consideration of geometrical truths, professing his intention to select those which were of paramount importance, since it was obvious that the number of possible problems in geometry was infinite.

'Illae (veritates),' he says, 'sunt eligendae quae possunt vocari radices et elementa respectu ramorum et foliorum, quorum fructus vadit in infinitum.' Proof is given in this part of the work that Bacon was acquainted with the geometry of Apollonius as well as with that of Euclid. After defining the cone ('pyramis rotunda') he mentions its three sections, presenting curves of a different form from the circle, one of which was of use in the construction of mirrors capable of rendering rays convergent to a point. He promises to deal with these curves later in the work.

On the whole, so far as the fragment of his mathematical work preserved to us enables us to judge, it would seem that Bacon had made himself acquainted with the highest mathematics of his

ASTROLOGY 83

time; though no evidence is forthcoming to show that he contributed personally to the advance of the science, otherwise than by strongly insisting on its culture, and by pointing out new fields for its practical application, in the better government of the Church, and in the development of industry. His interest, like that of Galileo, lay in applied rather than in abstract mathematics. Whether the study of equations as carried on by the Italian algebraists of the fourteenth and fifteenth centuries would have interested him is doubtful. But he would have eagerly welcomed the invention of logarithms, as facilitating the construction of astronomical tables.

VI. BACON'S ASTROLOGY [1]

The transition from Mathematics to Physics supplies the best opportunity for a few remarks on the subject of Bacon's Astrology, on which something is also said in a note to vol. i, p. 269.[2]

[1] [A recently discovered fragment of the *Op. Tert.* shows that the astrological treatise on pp. 376–403 of vol. i of Dr Bridges' ed. of the *Op. Maj.* was not originally a part of that work, but belonged to the *Op. Minus.* See p. xvii of Mr Little's *Op. Tert.*, 1912.]

[2] ['It has often been remarked that Roger Bacon was supported by Albertus Magnus, by Aquinas, and, indeed, all the best thinkers of his time in his conviction of the truth of astrology.

Bacon dwelt frequently and emphatically on the unity and the correlation of the sciences. In passing from Mathematics to the direct study of nature, he found a connecting link in the imaginary science of Astrology, which he studied zealously. That the fixed stars and the planets exercised a powerful influence on all earthly things, and not least on man; that the careful observation of their position at the moment of birth would do much to reveal the hidden springs of character, and make it possible to form a forecast of the ensuing life; that the influences radiating from them acted with greater or less potency according

To a believer in a limited and spherical universe with a terrestrial centre, nothing could seem more valid as a working hypothesis for explaining physical changes on the earth's surface than that alterations of the directions in which the planets were seen should be followed by corresponding alterations of terrestrial objects. The combinations of planetary bodies as seen in conjunction, in opposition, or in intermediate positions, offered a wide field of speculation, which became practically boundless when to the apparent relation of these bodies to one another were added their apparent relations (also ever varying) with the fixed stars. Human and terrestrial events, complicated as they might be, were paralleled by equal complication in the play of celestial forces. It may be said on the whole that so far from belief in astrology being a reproach to Bacon and his contemporaries, to have disbelieved in it would have been in the thirteenth century a sign of intellectual weakness. It conformed to the first law of Comte's *philosophia prima* as being the best hypothesis of which the ascertained phenomena admitted.'—*Op. Maj.*, vol. i, p. 269 *n.*]

ASTROLOGY

as the course of the rays was perpendicular or oblique, and that in this way an explanation could be given of climate, temperament, and of the thousand complex chances and changes of mortal life, was a belief firmly held by Bacon, and it operated powerfully over his whole view of man's position in the world. He has been much reproached for holding it; and it has been supposed to be an explanation, if not an excuse, for the disastrous repression exercised over him by his superiors, and for the popular discredit attaching to his name.

But this would be an entire misconception of the beliefs current in Bacon's time. The influence of the stars over human life was a belief almost universally held by all instructed men from the thirteenth to the sixteenth century; and abundant traces of it are visible throughout the seventeenth, not to speak of still later times. The *Divina Commedia* is full of it. Beatrice, admonishing Dante at her first meeting with him in the Earthly Paradise, speaks of the rich endowment with which he came into the world,

'Per ovra delle ruote magne,
Che drizzan ciascun seme ad alcun fine,
Secondo che le stelle son compagne.'[1]

---

[1] *Purgat.*, xxx, 109-11. Even more significant is the passage, *Parad.*, viii, 127-32 :—

By Dante's master in theology, Thomas Aquinas, the reality of astrological influences is laid down with perfect clearness in *Summa Theologiae* (Pars 1, quaest. 115, art. 3 and 4). In the first instance the question is put whether heavenly bodies are a cause of things that take place in terrestrial bodies. This, after the usual statement of reasons, for and against, is answered emphatically in the affirmative. 'Celestial bodies causally affect all the varied motions of terrestrial bodies.'[1] The second question is: Are heavenly bodies a cause of human actions? The authoritative conclusion here is: Directly speaking, they are not, but indirectly they are.[2] 'Indirectly, and by accident, impressions of celestial bodies may reach intellect and will, since both intellect and will receive

> 'La circular natura, ch' è suggello
> Alla cera mortal, fa ben sua arte
> Ma non distingue l' un dall' altro ostello.
> Quinci addivien ch' Esaù si diparte
> Per seme da Jacób, e vien Quirino
> Da sì vil padre che si rende a Marte.'

[1] The words are: 'Corpora caelestia cum tantum mobilia sint secundum lationis motum, causa sunt omnium eorum quae in his corporibus inferioribus variis motibus aguntur.'

[2] 'Cum intellectus et voluntas, quae humanorum actuum principia sunt, corporeis organis vires alligatae minime sint; non possunt corpora ipsa caelestia humanorum actuum causae directe esse, sed indirecte, agendo per se in corpora quae ad utriusque potentiae opera conducunt.'

somewhat from inferior faculties which are bound up with bodily organs. A distinction is, however, to be made between will and intellect. The intellect is of necessity affected by the lower apprehensive faculties of imagination, thought, or memory, and when these are stirred, the intellect is stirred likewise. But the will does not of necessity follow the promptings of the lower appetite. For although the passions of anger and desire have a certain power of moving the will ; yet it remains in the power of will to follow passion or to repudiate it. Thus the influence of celestial bodies, so far as it produces change in the lower faculties, has to do rather with intellect than with will; and will is the proximate cause of human action.'

Finally Aquinas remarks that ' most men follow passions, which are motions of the sensitive appetite ; and with these heavenly bodies may have to do. For few are the wise who withstand such passions. And thus it is that astrologers may often foretell truly ; but for the most part rather in general than in special, since nothing hinders any one man from withstanding passions by free will. Hence, astrologers themselves say that the wise man governs the stars, in so far, namely, as he governs his own passions.' Farther on, in *Prima Secundae* (quaest. ix, art. 5), this subject is again discussed. The question asked is, 'Can will be influenced by a heavenly body?' The conclusion is, 'Since will is a faculty absolutely immaterial and incorporeal, it can only be influenced by heavenly bodies indirectly.' And in his comment Aquinas observes, 'So far as will is influenced by any outward object, it can evidently be influenced by heavenly bodies: since all external bodies, which, when presented to the senses, move will, and even the very organs of sensitive faculties, are influenced by the motions of the heavens. But there is no direct action of heavenly bodies upon the will. For the will, as Aristotle says (*De Anima*, lib. iii) resides in reason; and reason is a power of the soul not bound to a bodily organ. . . . On the other hand,' he adds, 'sensitive appetite is the function (actus) of a bodily organ. Wherefore nothing hinders impressions of celestial bodies from rendering some men apt to anger, or to lust, or to some passion of this kind; and thus from natural complexion many men follow passions, and wise men alone withstand them. And so, in a general way, are verified those things that are foretold of the actions of men in accordance with the consideration of heavenly bodies.'

Now the view taken by Bacon coincides precisely with that of Aquinas. Confusion, he says (*Op. Maj.*, p. 239), had arisen in the matter in consequence of the equivocal meaning of the word *Mathematics*, sometimes held to be derived from μαντική, sometimes from μάθησις. The characteristic, he says, of false mathematics was to assert that through the powers of the constellations all things took place of necessity. No place was left for contingent matter, for judgment, for free will. Such a view of nature was condemned not only by theologians but by philosophers. Aristotle and Plato, Cicero and Pliny, Avicenna and Albumazar, were unanimous in holding that free will remained uncoerced by the motions of heavenly bodies. 'True mathematicians and astrologers lay down no necessity, no infallibility, in their predictions of contingent events. . . . What they do is to consider the way in which the body may be affected by celestial things, and the way in which the body may act upon the mind in private affairs or public, always without prejudice to the freedom of the will. For although the reasonable soul is not coerced to any future actions, yet it may be strongly stirred and induced, so as freely to will those things towards which celestial force may incline it; as we see men in community taking counsel, or through fear or love, and feelings of this kind, freely choosing what before they would not, though not forced to do so ; like the sailor who to save himself from drowning throws precious merchandise into the sea. We see, indeed, that impressions from things on earth may so act upon sense as to stir men to will what before they had no care for, so that they take no account of death or disgrace or fear, if only they accomplish their desire, as with those who see and hear the onset of their enemies, and are borne onwards at all hazards to avenge themselves. . . . Far more potent than the impressions of earthly things are those of the heavenly upon bodily organs, which being strongly moved, men are led on to actions of which they had not thought before, yet always with full reservation of the freedom of the will.'

There are perhaps few fictitious creeds for the origin of which it is so easy to account as for the belief that the position of the planets with regard to one another and to the constellations of the zodiac were of significance to man and his environment. With populations whose religion was astrolatric rather than polytheistic, taking shape in worship of the heavens rather than that of invisible but manlike gods, astrology would be an easy and almost inevitable deduction from their creed. The immense majority of the Asiatic

ASTROLOGY

populations, whether Semitic or Mongol, were, unlike the Indians and the Greeks, not polytheists but astrolaters. When the Arabs received and enlarged their inheritance of Ptolemaic astronomy, their astrologic beliefs, far from being dissipated, were strongly confirmed. Of the seven wanderers of the sky, the influence on earthly things of two, the Sun and the Moon, was too obvious to be disputed. The one swayed the tides, the other brought summer and winter. Why should the rest be supposed inert? Was it not probable that the successive and infinitely varying connexion of each of them, singly or combined, with the fixed groups of the starry vault, indicated changes or tendencies to change here below which careful and prolonged study might at last interpret?

So it was that with the growth of knowledge, and with increasing strength of the conviction that all nature was under the dominion of fixed laws, astrology came to be regarded as the key to the understanding of all that was specially contingent and variable in man's environment; the phenomena of temperament and of disease; the revolutions of states, and even of religions. The boundary of its lawful application was drawn differently by different thinkers. Apart from charlatans and miracle-mongers, few stretched it farther than Bacon. But by him, as strictly as by Aquinas, the saving clause, 'salva arbitrii libertate,' was always added. Outside influences might suggest motive and kindle passion; they could never trench upon the sacred domain of the freedom of the will.[1]

What is strange is not that the belief in the

[1] Comte has pointed out (*Philosophie Positive*, vol. iii, pp. 273-80, ed. Littré) that in order to appreciate astrology with any approach to justice, it is needful to keep steadily in view the very real connexion between the sciences of astronomy and biology. On the relations of mass and of distance between the sun and earth, involving as they do the familiar facts of weight, equilibrium of fluids, temperature, life on our planet is obviously dependent. If we consider the period and velocity of the earth's rotation, the degree of ellipticity of her orbit, the angle at which the axis of rotation is inclined to the plane of the orbit, the same truth is impressed upon us even more strongly. 'In the early stages of the human mind these connecting links between astronomy and biology were studied from a very different point of view; but at least they were studied and not left out of sight, as is the common tendency in our own time under the restricting influence of a nascent and incomplete positivism. Beneath the chimerical beliefs of the old philosophy in the physiological influence of the stars, there lay a strong though confused recognition of the truth that the facts of life were in some way dependent on the solar system. Like all primitive inspirations of man's intelligence this feeling needed rectification by positive science, but not destruction; though unhappily in science, as in politics, it is often hard to reorganize without some brief period of overthrow.' This was written in 1836. Much has been done since by Mr Herbert Spencer and others to familiarize the European mind with the dependence of life on its astronomical conditions. But the injustice in our historical judgment of mediæval astrology still remains.

convergence of stellar influences towards the central point of a closed universe should have arisen, but that it should so long and so persistently have survived the discovery that the universe was not closed but boundless. That Francis Bacon, who rejected or doubted the Copernican theory, should have retained his belief in astrology is not surprising. But we should have expected that with men like Kepler and Campanella it would have vanished like the morning mist. Yet it was not so.

VII. THE PROPAGATION OF FORCE

Bacon's views of stellar influences must be taken in connexion with his speculations as to the transmission of force through space. These are set forth briefly in the second and third Distinctions of the fourth part of the *Opus Majus*; and more in detail in the special treatise *De Multiplicatione Specierum*,[1] which in this edition [of the *Op. Maj.*] is given as an appendix.

[1] ['The scholastic style of this work contrasts strongly with that of the *Opus Majus*, which, as we know, was a *Persuasio Praeambula*. It has been less studied than Bacon's other works, not so much from its difficulty as from the notion that it was a mere recast of Aristotelian Physics, and from the further notion that Aristotelian Physics were not worth studying. Both of

'Species' is the word chosen by Bacon to express the emanation of force which he conceives to be continually proceeding from every bodily object in all directions. Body of every kind is endowed with force which indeed is identical with its substance or essence. The first result of this force, resembling it in character, is its species, otherwise called likeness, or image, or intention, or impression. In other words, body is a centre of activity or force radiating in every direction. Species is the first result of this force, the ray proceeding from the body. Tracing back this doctrine to its origin, we find it expounded in the fourth book of the *De Rerum Natura* of Lucretius, in Diogenes Laërtius' account of the system of Epicurus, and in the traces that remain to us of older philosophers, notably of Democritus. Aristotle, in his short treatise on divination by dreams, alludes to the theory of Democritus that

these positions, I venture to think, will be abandoned when the same attention shall have been given to the history of science that has been given during the last half-century to other departments of evolution. What lifts Bacon's discussions upon force to a higher level than that of barren dialectical debate is, that they were animated by constant reference to a living and growing science due to the later Greeks, and still more to the Arabians, the science of Optics, including the study of the organs of vision and perception no less than that of the force acting on them. For Bacon the radiation of light was a type of all other radiant forces.'—*Op. Maj.*, vol. ii, p. 552 *n.*]

PROPAGATION OF FORCE 95

εἴδωλα and ἀπόρροιαι were continually emitted from objects which in the stillness of the night were capable of affecting the sleeper. By Epicurus, in his letter to Herodotus quoted in his biography by Diogenes Laërtius, the theory is more fully detailed. 'There are moulds,' he says, 'corresponding to all solid bodies preserving the same shape and arrangement as these bodies which emanate from them, and are conveyed through space with incredible velocity. These may be called images. Their flow from bodies is continuous so that they are not separately perceived.' The description of them by Lucretius is more definite and better known. 'Pictures of things and thin shapes are emitted from things off their surface; these are like films or may each be named a rind, because each image bears an appearance and form like to the thing, whatever it is, from whose body it is shed and wanders forth' (*De Rerum Natura*, iv. 40, Monro's translation). And again, 'Many idols are begotten in a short time, so that the birth of such things is with good reason named a rapid one. And as the sun must send forth many rays of light in a short time in order that all things may be continually filled with it, so also for a like reason there must be carried away from things in a moment of time idols of things, many in number, in many ways, in all directions round.

... As soon as ever the brightness of water is set down in the open air, if the heaven is starry, in a moment the clear radiant constellations of ether imaged in the water correspond to those in the heaven. Now do you see in what a moment of time an image drops down from the borders of heaven to the borders of earth' (iv, 159 and 211). He goes on to explain that not the sense of sight only, but all the senses, are affected by these emanations.

But it would be an entire misapprehension of Bacon's views as to the propagation of force to identify them with the crude physics of Epicurus.

In the first place, Bacon wholly rejects the notion that the species is something emitted from the agent, or acting body (*De Mult. Spec.*, pp. 432-8). If it were so, the agent would be weakened and ultimately destroyed by the emission, which is not the case. Nor again does the agent create the species out of nothing. Nor does it collect the species from surrounding space and send it on into the body on which action takes place—the patient. Nor, as some have supposed, does the agent impress the patient as with a seal.

What happens is that the agent stimulates the potential activity of the matter of the patient. The species is generated out of the matter acted on. 'Fit species de potentia activa materiae

PROPAGATION OF FORCE

patientis.' The agent acts on the first part of the body of the patient, and stimulates its latent energy to the generation of the species. That part thus transmuted acts on the part next succeeding; and so the action proceeds (*De Mult. Spec.*, p. 457).

While the agent acts on the patient, the patient reacts on the agent. 'Omne agens physice patitur et transmutatur insimul dum agit, et omne patiens physice agit' (*De Mult. Spec.*, p. 439). Heavenly bodies as they act on one another, so do they receive emanations of force from terrestrial bodies. Not that they are so affected by them as to be destroyed, being incorruptible. Nevertheless there is in this way an interchange of force between all parts of the universe (p. 448).

The ray, or species, is of corporeal nature; but this corporeal nature is not distinct from that of the medium; it is generated from the substance of the medium, and is continually re-formed out of successive portions of the medium occurring in the line along which the force is propagated (p. 504). If wind is driving the air transversely to the line of force, this in no way affects this line. The species is formed and re-formed from particles of the medium presented in the line of propagation, and from no others.

Finally, the propagation of rays occupies time

(vol. ii, pp. 67–72 and 525–9), though its velocity is such that the time occupied in passing through so vast a space as the diameter of the universe is imperceptible to sense.

It will be seen from the foregoing how wide is the divergence between Democritean and Baconian physics. Though Bacon retains the word 'species' in his theory, the word has almost entirely lost the significance attached to it by Lucretius. We are no longer dealing with the notion that bodies emit from their surface films or moulds which are transmitted through space. Like the word 'ray,' which is retained by the modern physicist who accepts the undulatory theory, 'species' for Bacon has become a mere word to denote the propagation of force in certain definite directions. Indeed the multiplication of species as defined by him has much in common with the undulatory theory. He formally rejects the contrasted theory of emission.[1] The species, like the wave, is a motion or change in successive portions of the aerial or ethereal medium; occupying time in its transit; propagated so long as the medium be homogeneous, in direct lines;

[1] ['With regard to the part taken by the medium in the transmission of force, it will be seen that Bacon's view is far more nearly akin to the views of Descartes, Young, or Faraday than to the emission theory of Newton. Action at a distance was as inconceivable to him as to Aristotle, and to most modern physicists.'—*Op. Maj.*, vol. ii, p. 431 *n*.]

PROPAGATION OF FORCE 99

liable to deflexion when the medium alters its character.

In Bacon's theory of the radiation of forces two very important points are to be noted. The first is his clear grasp of the principle that time was occupied in their transmission. He discusses, in the passages already cited, the view of Aristotle and others that the propagation of light differed from that of sound and odour by being instantaneous.[1] We might admit, Aristotle had said, that light could pass through short spaces without our being able to detect any interval of time during the passage. But when light passes from east to west through the universe, the space is so vast that if time were occupied we could not fail to detect it. Bacon's conception of the subject is far more scientific. Our inability to perceive minute intervals of time is no evidence, he said, for their non-existence. Imperceptible time, he remarks, has many degrees. There is, first, the interval of time

[1] ['This subject is also discussed in *De Mult. Spec.*, iv, cap. 3. The present chapter and that which follows are specially interesting as showing the independent manner in which Bacon criticized his authorities, Aristotle included, while allowing due weight to their objections. He dissents from the conclusion of Aristotle and Al-Kindi that the propagation of light was instantaneous. He adopts the conclusion of Alhazen, while explaining that some of Alhazen's reasons for it were fallacious. Bacon's own reasoning on the subject is remarkable as an anticipation of the discovery made by Roemer in 1675.'—*Op. Maj.*, vol. ii, p. 68 *n.*]

occupied by a single propagation of force (or, as we should say, undulation) followed by the interval of rest before the next propagation begins. Take such a multiple of that interval as would suffice for the whole distance between the extremities of a diameter of the universe, and that multiple may still remain below the limits of our power of perception. It is interesting to compare with this passage the speculations of the second Bacon on the same subject (*Nov. Org.*, ii, 46). Francis Bacon had formed the conjecture that the transit of light from the stars occupied time. But he did not grasp this conjecture with the same firmness as Roger Bacon, and he follows it up with ingenious arguments which explain it away.

Radiant force, in Bacon's view, proceeded independently of man's power to perceive it. Opaque bodies, he observes, offered resistance to the passage of a luminous ray (*De Mult. Spec.*, p. 478; see also *Op. Maj.*, vol. i, p. 114). But 'no substance is so dense as altogether to prevent rays from passing. Matter is common to all things, and thus there is no substance on which the action involved in the passage of a ray may not produce a change. Thus it is that rays of heat and sound penetrate through the walls of a vessel of gold or brass. It is said by Boethius that a lynx's eye will pierce through thick walls.

In this case the wall would be permeable to visual rays. In any case there are many dense bodies which altogether interfere with the visual and other senses of man, so that rays cannot pass with such energy as to produce an effect on human sense, and yet nevertheless rays do really pass, though without our being aware of it.' Recent discoveries[1] have given significance to this remarkable passage ; which, not merely to his contemporaries, but to succeeding generations, must have seemed in the highest degree fantastical.

VIII. BACON'S OPTICS

The most striking illustration of laws governing the transit of force through space was obviously to be looked for in the science of Optics (*Perspectiva*). The fifth section of the *Opus Majus*, amounting to about one-fifth of the whole, is devoted to this science ; and much supplemental matter is added in the treatise *De Multiplicatione Specierum*. Optics had been studied by the Greeks to much purpose. The works of Euclid, Theon, and Ptolemy were translated into Arabic, and were carefully studied by Arabian men of

[1] [Dr Bridges here alludes to the Röntgen or X-rays discovered in 1895.]

science, notably by Abû 'Alî al Hasan ibn al Hasan ibn Alhaitam, better known to Occidentals under the name of Alhazen. Their principal results are embodied in Bacon's work.

Euclid, or the author passing under his name,[1] was aware that light proceeded in straight lines, and that visual rays were reflected from plane mirrors in such a way that the angles made with the surface on each side were equal. He conceived the assemblage of rays as a cone having its apex in the eye, and its base in the boundary of the object seen: thus the apparent magnitude of the object depended on the magnitude of the angle of the cone. Thence followed the ordinary principles of perspective, as that of equal magnitudes at unequal distances; those nearer to the eye appeared larger, and so on. In the *Catoptrica* (attributed to Euclid, but probably due to Theon), from the equality of the angles of reflexion and incidence in plane mirrors was deduced the convergence of rays falling on a concave speculum.

[1] Heiberg, in his recent edition [1895] of Euclid's *Optica* (forming the seventh volume of the complete edition of Euclid, edited by Heiberg and Menge), remarks (p. xxix of *Prolegomena*), 'Optica, qualia hic e codice Vindobonensi maxime primo loco repetivimus, Euclidis esse, non est, cur dubitemus. Sed cum recentiores tantum exstent codices, mirum non est, locos nonnullos tam corruptos esse, ut verba Euclidis restitui nequeant.'

OPTICS

Ptolemy[1] carried the science much further than Euclid. To the study of reflected light he added that of refraction. The chief interest of his work lies in the application to the subject of the experimental method, an instance of it unique, if we except the Pythagorean experiments in acoustics, in the history of Greek science. Using an extremely simple but ingenious apparatus, he discovered, not merely that the luminous ray in passing from one medium to another was deflected, but, within certain limits, he ascertained the amount of deflexion and its dependence on two distinct factors, the angle of incidence, and the nature of the two media concerned.[2] Ptolemy distinctly describes and explains the error introduced by refraction into astronomical observations. The

---

[1] On Ptolemy's *Optics* there is a very interesting chapter in Delambre's *Astronomie Ancienne*, vol. ii, pp. 411-432, ed. 1817. (See also a note on p. li of Preface to vol. i, which modifies some of his conclusions.) All our knowledge of Ptolemy's optical work comes from an imperfect Latin translation from the Arabic made in the twelfth century by Admiral Eugenio of Sicily. There are late MSS. of this work in Paris and in the Bodleian Library. But Govi's recent edition [Turin, 1885] is from a much older MS. in the Ambrosian Library of Milan.

[2] ['In his fifth chapter, which is the most original of the treatise, Ptolemy gives tables of refraction for different angles from 10° to 80° for rays passing from air to water, from water to air, and from water to glass; one of the earliest attempts to deal quantitatively with experimental research.'—*Op. Maj.*, vol. ii, p. 473 *n.*]

fact that in his great astronomical treatise there is no mention of refraction had led to the conclusion that the *Almagest* and the *Optics* must be attributed to distinct authors. The *Optics*, however, may be a later work. We know it only from a translation from the Arabic into Latin, made in the twelfth century; it has been recently edited by Gilberto Govi, of Turin. The researches of Euclid, Ptolemy, and others on Optics, engaged the attention of the Arabian schools from an early period. Their knowledge of the subject is summed up in the work of Alhazen, whose remarkable work, *Thesaurus Opticae*, written perhaps in the eleventh century, was translated in the twelfth into Latin; as Jourdain thinks, by Gerard of Cremona, the translator of Ptolemy's *Almagest*. Alhazen was the writer on whom Roger Bacon principally relied; though he makes frequent use of the optical treatises of Euclid, Ptolemy, Tideus, and Al-Kindi.

Alhazen's work is copious in the extreme; in some parts extremely tedious. Its value as a document in the history of science is, however, very great. It consists of seven books. The first begins with a brief exposition of the nature of light and colour, and proceeds to explain the anatomy of the organs of vision. The second deals with the function of vision and with the

OPTICS

physiology of perception. The third, with imperfections and illusions incident to vision. The fourth, fifth, and sixth are devoted to the subject of reflexion.[1] Seven kinds of mirrors are discussed, plane, spherical, cylindrical, and conical; the convex and concave forms of the three last being separately considered. The multiplication and position of the images formed is treated with inordinate length, but with such geometrical skill as to secure for him an abiding place in the history of pure, no less than of applied, mathematics. 'His investigation,' says Cantor (*Gesch. der Math.*, vol. i, p. 677), 'of the problem : In a spherical concave mirror, to find the point from which an object of given position will be reflected

[1] ['The fourth book of Alhazen, cap. 3, gives a very detailed account of the construction of the apparatus for testing the equality of the angles of reflexion and incidence. The cases of plane, spherical, cylindrical, and conical mirrors are separately investigated. (See also Vitello, lib. v, 9, which is almost exactly copied from Alhazen, though as usual without acknowledgment.) The description illustrates the extreme care taken by the Arab investigators in the construction of their instruments. The orifices in the armillary through which the rays were admitted were half a barleycorn, or one-sixth of an inch in diameter. But for more precise investigation the orifice was closed with wax, and a smaller opening made through the central point. Further, a comparison was made between the ray passing from the orifice in the armillary to the point of reflexion through a closed tube and a similar ray unconfined in its passage. It was noted that the reflected ray was found feebler in the first case, though the direction was unaltered.'—*Op. Maj.*, vol. ii, p. 483 *n*.]

to an eye of given position, is one which, analytically handled, leads to an equation of the fourth degree.' Alhazen solved it, as Govi remarks (Ptol., *Opt.*, p. xix), by the use of an hyperbola.

The seventh book of the *Thesaurus Opticae* deals with refraction. A very elaborate description is given of the instrument for measuring it, part of which Bacon quotes. Moreover, an attempt is made to explain the cause of refraction which is substantially identical with Bacon's, as may be seen by comparison of Alhazen (lib. vii, 8) with *De Multiplicatione Specierum* (Pars II, cap. 3). The apparatus for measuring the angle of refraction, which was more accurately designed than that of Ptolemy, enabled a series of observations to be made of the angle of refraction, in different media, on which the true law of the variations of refraction at different angles and in different media might ultimately be based. Vitello,[1] Bacon's con-

---

[1] Of Vitello, or Witelo, very little is known. He describes himself in his dedication to William of Morbeta (identified by Cantor as William of Moerbeke) as filius Thuringorum et Polonorum. In lib. x, 74 of his work he speaks of Poland as his country, and other passages (x, 42 and 67) show that he travelled in Italy. His work on Optics was edited with great care, and with many emendations, by Risner, and published at Bale in 1572 in the same volume that contained Risner's edition of Alhazen. Indeed, it may be described with little exaggeration as a revised edition of Alhazen's work; with many additions certainly from other authors, but with none of those acknow-

OPTICS

temporary, drew up a table of refractions, as Ptolemy had done before him, for the three media of air, water, and glass. It was soon seen that the angle of refraction did not vary in accordance with the angle of incidence. But more than three centuries were to pass before the discovery of the law of sines, that is to say, the law that the ratio of the sines of the angles of incidence and refraction is constant for refraction in the same medium, was effected by Snell and Descartes.

It might seem, at first sight, that the optical work of Bacon was little more than an abridgment of that of Alhazen.[1] But this view would render Bacon but scanty justice. Problems of great importance were indicated by him which Alhazen had entirely neglected. In considering

ledgments of his principal teacher of which Bacon's *Perspectiva* is full. Vitello's tables of refraction have excited much admiration. They prove, however, on careful examination to be an almost exact repetition of those of Ptolemy. Whether Bacon and Vitello ever came into contact there is no evidence to show. Bacon was always ready to mention the sources of his knowledge. Not so Vitello. If he borrowed from Bacon, he would not have said so.

[1] It must be owned that where Bacon differed from Alhazen, the advantage was not always on his side. Alhazen contended vigorously against the view of the older oculists that vision took place by visual force issuing from the eye, maintaining that the ray proceeded to the eye from the object. Bacon (*Op. Maj.*, vol. ii, pp. 49-53) makes a fruitless attempt to conciliate these opposite views.

the point on the axis of a spherical concave mirror to which rays were reflected, Bacon remarks that this point would be different for rays reflected from each concentric circle traced round the centre of the mirror. Such a mirror failed therefore to produce complete convergence of rays. For such convergence the curvature must be other than spherical, it must be that produced by the rotation of a conic section.[1]

Bacon, moreover, is distinguished from the Arabian optical writers, and from other investigators of his own time, by his sedulous endeavours to turn the discovery of the laws of reflexion and refraction to practical account. Neither in Alhazen nor in Vitello is there any attempt to construct instruments for the purpose of increasing the power of vision. With Bacon this object was always held steadily in view. Of the simple

[1] ['From this passage, and from the last paragraph of this chapter, we see that Bacon knew that by using parabolic mirrors all the reflected rays would be concentrated in a single focus. Nevertheless he exaggerates the defects of the spherical mirror, from a small portion of the surface of which all the rays are practically focussed in a single point. He does not seem to distinguish the case of parallel rays, proceeding from a distant source of light, from that of divergent rays, when the source of light is near.

'Alhazen's work shows no acquaintance with parabolic mirrors. But their properties and the mode of constructing them are minutely described by Witelo (*Vitellonis Opticae*, lib. ix, cap. 39-44).'—*Op. Maj.*, vol. ii, p. 487 *n.*]

OPTICS

microscope he had a perfectly clear conception. His scientific imagination played freely with the possibilities of bringing distant objects near, and of indefinitely magnifying minute objects, by giving suitable directions to refracted rays, and by the use of appropriate media. It would be, however, an entire exaggeration of his achievements to speak of him as the inventor of the telescope. No evidence is forthcoming for his having effected the simple combination of two convex lenses, or of a convex with a concave lens, on which the power of telescopic vision depends. All that can be claimed for him is that he was the first definitely and explicitly to bring the problem forward, leaving it for after generations to solve. In truth, his conception of an optical image, as constructed by the assemblage of foci of rays proceeding from each point of the object magnified, though in the main correct, was not always clearly grasped. Of the distinction between virtual and real images, his notion was entirely in default.

Nor, again, had Bacon a clear conception of the conditions of distinct vision. He examined to much better purpose than Alhazen had done the structures of the eye; and he was aware of the refraction produced by the curved surface of the cornea, and by the doubly convex crystalline lens. But what he failed to grasp was the necessity of a clear image of the object defined on the retina; that image being produced by the focussing on the retina of rays proceeding from each point of the object.[1] The phenomena of accommodation, produced by the action of the ciliary muscle, which, by altering the curvature of the lens, enables rays from near objects to be accurately focussed, were unknown to him. But this is only to say that he had not anticipated the physiological knowledge of the nineteenth century.[2]

It must always be borne in mind that, in Bacon's view, the radiation of light through space did not stand alone. It was a type of other radiant activities, such as colour (then supposed to be distinct from, though dependent on, light), heat,

[1] ['It is clear from the foregoing, and especially from the discussion illustrated by fig. 69, that Bacon had a clear conception of an image as resulting from a series of points, each point in the *res visa* being separately refracted. But he did not apprehend the necessity for focussing an image of the object on the retina, as was so clearly demonstrated, nearly four centuries afterwards, by Descartes in the fifth discourse of his *Dioptrique*.'—*Op. Maj.*, vol. ii, p. 159 *n*.]

[2] ['Fantastic as Bacon's explanation of Presbyopia may be, it should be remembered how very recent is the true explanation. Not till midway in the last century was it suggested (by Porterfield) that accommodation of sight to near objects depended on an increase in the curvature of the lens produced by contraction of the ciliary muscle; and that weakness of the muscle and rigidity of the lens came on with age. Knowledge of the precise mechanism of the process was reserved for our own time.'—*Op. Maj.*, vol. ii, p. 86 *n*.]

sound, and odour. (With regard to sound, however, certain reserves were made.) It is interesting to note Bacon's handling of an important problem, not to be solved but by a more potent calculus than any in his possession, how these various actions, crossing one another's paths in their passage through space, retained their distinctness.[1]

[1] ['The problem discussed by Bacon in the two foregoing chapters is one that presented great difficulties to natural philosophers, not merely in antiquity and in the Middle Ages, but down to a period at least as late as the middle of the eighteenth century. Assuming that light, heat, or sound were conveyed to our senses by progressive disturbances of the medium interposed between the sensory organ and the object apprehended (and this, as will be seen, was Bacon's view), how was it that these lines of disturbance proceeding simultaneously from different objects or from different points in the same object did not produce confusion when they intersected? The explanation offered by some that these lines of radiating force were of immaterial and spiritual nature, and therefore like other spiritual things had no relation to space, Bacon rejects as an untenable evasion of the difficulty: one of the barren solutions characteristic of scholastic logic when unimpregnated by scientific research. (Cf. *De Mult. Spec.*, iii, 2.) His own solution was that the line of force which impinged vertically on the sense-organ was so much more effectual than those which fell upon it obliquely as to neutralize them. The solution was at least real, so far as it went; though of course entirely insufficient. But it was much to have conceived distinctly the importance of the problem. For a better solution the world had to wait until Daniel Bernoulli solved the problem of the coexistence of small oscillations; proving that the oscillations due to different causes went on as though each took place separately. (*Cf.* Comte, *Philosophie Positive*, i, 530, ed. Littré.)'—*Op. Maj.*, vol. ii, p. 46 *n*.]

IX. BACON'S ALCHEMY

It will be remembered [p. 58] that among the various branches of knowledge regarded by Bacon as falling under the head of Natural Science was Barology (Scientia ponderum). The treatise of Jordanus Nemorarius, *De Ponderibus*, to which reference is made in the *Opus Majus* (vol. i, p. 169), had perhaps suggested the treatment of the phenomena of gravity as a distinct branch of science. No treatise by Bacon upon this subject, so far as I am aware, is extant; and the few remarks in the fourth section of the *Opus Majus* (pp. 167–174) contain all that we know of his speculations on the theory of gravitation.

Nor is anything known to us of the way in which Bacon treated, if indeed he ever attempted, the science which he called 'Agricultura,' which, as we have seen, was intended to include the study of living bodies, vegetable and animal. But the case is otherwise with the science regarded by him as preparatory to the study of life, 'Alkimia Speculativa.' On the subject of Alchemy, very little is said in the *Opus Majus*; and the omission was supplied in the provisional way, which alone was possible under the hurry of compilation to satisfy Pope Clement's

ALCHEMY

orders,[1] by the *Opus Minus*, the first of the two appendages to that work. Unfortunately the only text of the *Opus Minus* which we possess has come down to us, not merely incomplete, but in so corrupt a state as to render it often very difficult to decipher Bacon's meaning. Enough remains, however, to show the large and comprehensive spirit in which Bacon regarded the subject.[2]

The contempt expressed in much modern writing for mediæval alchemy might be well retorted on its authors. Admit that some prosecutors of the occult art were deceivers as well as deceived, and that others were impelled by wild

---

[1] ['Bacon sent to Clement IV four treatises on this subject: two were inserted in the *Opus Minus*, a third was sent separately by the hand of John, and is unknown. The fourth has recently been discovered by Professor Duhem appended to the *Opus Tertium*. It consists of three chapters: *De enigmatibus Alkimie, De expositione enigmatum Alkimie, De clavibus Alkimie.*' —App. to *Comp. Stud. Theol.*, p. 89, ed. Little, 1911.]

[2] ['Other works of Bacon on Alchemy are (1) *Speculum Alchemiae*, printed in 1541 and translated both into French and English; (2) *De secretis operibus artis et naturae* reprinted as an Appendix to Brewer's work; (3) The treatise *De retardandis senectutis accidentibus* already spoken of; (4) *Sanioris medicinae magistri Rogeri Baconis angli de arte chymiae scripta*, printed in 1603, and sometimes spoken of under the title given to it in the second edition of 1620, of *Thesaurus chemicus*.

'For the position of Alchemy in the history of science, the remarks of Comte (*Philosophie Positive*, vol. vi, p. 209, ed. Littré) may be consulted with advantage.'—*Op. Maj.*, vol. ii, p. 215 *n*.]

hopes of gain, has the pursuit of physical science in modern times been wholly free from similar taints? Electricity applied to medicine has been a fertile field for impostors. And will anyone maintain that the pursuit of chemistry has not been stimulated by hopes of industrial profit? Yet such things are not allowed to cast a shade on the names of a Lavoisier, a Dalton, or a Faraday. Alchemy was chemistry in its prescientific period. Under the guidance of hypotheses which were not nearly so wild or crude as they at first appear, it attacked, like the true science which gradually grew from it, the important problem of the transmutation of matter by artificial agencies. It took for granted that metals were compound bodies, the elements of which might be separated and recomposed. This was no unreasonable supposition. Indeed, until modern spectrology had shown that the vapour of many metals existed undecomposed in the intense heat of the sun's atmosphere, there was no adequate reason for abandoning the attempt to decompose them. It would be hard to find in alchemy any conjecture more baseless than that of Phlogiston, the subtle spirit of flame, the loss of which by combustion made the oxide heavier than the metal. Yet Priestley accepted this hypothesis, and a Lavoisier was needed to destroy it.

ALCHEMY

Alkimia, as conceived by Bacon, fell into two great divisions—speculative and operative. Under the latter was included the metallurgy of the gold-seekers, and generally all the practical and industrial processes pursued, with more or less wisdom, by men who had a definite purpose in view—the transmutation of metals, the discovery of the philosopher's egg, or the *elixir vitae*. But Bacon was one of the few who saw that the empirical proceedings of the honest mystics or scheming charlatans, who were toiling at their royal road to wealth or longevity, covered speculations of a far deeper kind; the study of the transition of matter from the four Aristotelian elements, through increasing degrees of complexity, up to the highly compound forms exhibited by organized bodies. The 'Alkimia Speculativa' of Bacon was, indeed, not alchemy at all as commonly understood: it was nothing less than chemistry. 'Alkimia Speculativa,' he says, in the twelfth chapter of the *Opus Tertium*, 'treats of the generation of things from their elements, and of all inanimate things—as of the elements and liquids (*humores*) simple and compound; common stones, gems, and marbles; gold, and other metals; sulphur, salts, pigments, lapis lazuli, minium, and other colours; oils, bitumen, and very many other things—of which we find nothing in the books of Aristotle; nor are the natural philosophers or any of the Latins acquainted with these things. And being ignorant of them, they can know nothing of what follows in physics, that is, of the generation of animate things—as vegetables, animals, and man—because knowing not what is prior, they must remain ignorant of what is posterior. For the generation of men, and of brutes, and of plants, is from elemental and liquid substances, and is of like manner with the generation of inanimate things. Wherefore, through ignorance of this science, neither can natural philosophy, commonly so called, be known, nor the theory, and therefore neither the practice, of medicine; not merely because natural philosophy and theoretical medicine are necessary for the practice, but because all simple medicines are derived from inanimate things by this science.'

Of such fundamental truths of chemical science—as the composition of air and water, the theory of combustion, and the chemistry of carbon—he, like his contemporaries, was ignorant; but the ignorance was shared by the second Bacon with the first, and was not to be dissipated for five centuries. All that could be done in the meanwhile was to collect empirical information as to a few metals and their oxides, some of the principal

ALCHEMY

alkalis, acids, and salts. On all these things the Arab investigators, from Geber[1] downwards, had accumulated a considerable mass of material. It is not easy to define the results of each inquirer, owing to the prevalent habit of describing their procedure and results in mystical language. Self-defence against charges of magic and imposture was probably their motive. And that the danger was real, the history of Bacon's life suffices to show. His efforts to refute the charge of magic were incessant. In his treatise, *De Secretis Operibus Artis et Naturae et de nullitate Magiae*, he describes in detail the various procedures of the magician—sleight of hand, ventriloquism, pretended movements of inanimate things in dim light, the aid of accomplices, utterance of mysterious formulæ, invocation of spirits. We gather from the description that the lapse of six centuries has done little to change the character of charlatanism. But Bacon was aware that the charlatan was often in possession of valuable secrets. 'Many books are held to be magical,' he says, 'which are not really so, but which contain important truths; which are of this kind, and which are not, it is

[1] [There is, however, good reason to suppose that the Latin alchemical treatises formerly regarded as translations of the Arabic writings of Geber or Jaber are apocryphal, being probably original works dating from the thirteenth century. See vol. iii of Berthelot's *Chimie au moyen âge* (Paris, 1893).]

for the experience of the wise man to decide. If he find in them any result of natural or artificial forces (opus naturae vel artis), let him accept this ; otherwise let him reject them as worthless.' Bacon carefully guards himself against denial of the mystical force of words uttered under solemn conditions, as in the daily miracle of the Eucharist, or in the solemn invocations that protected the innocent when exposed to judicial ordeal. Such powers might be exerted for good as for evil; and the unlawful use of them was strictly and severely to be condemned.

But to whatever extent Bacon may have shared the illusions of his time with regard to the practical operations of alchemy, it is a striking proof of his scientific discernment that under the head of Speculative Alchemy he should have formed a clear, though distant, survey of chemical science as the intermediate link between Aristotelian Physics and the science of living bodies. As Physics followed on Mathematics, so did Chemistry, in Bacon's arrangement of the sciences, succeed Physics. After Chemistry came the study of living bodies [Agricultura], on which Bacon, while assigning to this science its natural place in the series, has said little or nothing. But on the study of plants and animals was based, under the name of Medicina, the study of the physical structure and functions of man. Here Bacon had for his guides, not Galen indeed, to whom his references are few, but Avicenna, Hali, and a host of Arabian professors of medical art, to whom Galen had supplied a very substantial foundation of anatomical and physiological knowledge. Bacon's short treatise, *De retardandis senectutis accidentibus*, to which reference is occasionally made in the *Opus Majus*, will sufficiently illustrate his views on this branch of science.[1]

[1] ['Bacon's treatise *De retardandis senectutis accidentibus* was translated into English in 1684 by a member of the College of Physicians, Dr Richard Brown, with notes on each chapter which not merely throw some light on the ingredients of his *elixir vitae*, but show, what is even more important, that to the medical mind four centuries after Roger Bacon, and half a century after Harvey, there was no *a priori* absurdity in the supposition that these ingredients were of value.

'The amazing want of relativity which still continues to vitiate historical judgments, and especially judgments in the history of science, suggests a caution analogous to that already given in the case of Astrology. Till the laws of living bodies were studied at the close of the eighteenth century by Bichat, Hunter, and others in the light of physical and chemical science, there was no antecedent improbability in supposing the possibility of indefinite prolongation of human life. Limits very different from those imagined by Bacon are now universally recognized; but it would be rash to say that all has been done that can be done to reach them. Again, as to the nature of the remedies. What physician thirty years ago, looking at a case of the disease now called myxoedema (which presents many of the appearances of premature old age), would not have smiled on hearing that it might be arrested or even cured by swallowing an extract

X. EXPERIMENTAL SCIENCE

Last among the series of the natural sciences comes that which Bacon denotes as 'Scientia Experimentalis.' The sample of it, for it can hardly be regarded as more than a sample, given in the sixth section of the *Opus Majus* indicates that it was connected in Bacon's mind with no special department of research, but was a general method used for the double purpose of controlling results already reached by mathematical procedure, and of stimulating new researches in fields not as yet opened to inquiry.[2]

In some respects this is the most original part of his work. Not that experiment was a new thing. Experiments without number had been made by man from the time of his first appearance on the planet. The Greeks towards the end of their marvellous scientific career had begun to use experiment in their investigations of natural truth.

from the thyroid gland of a sheep? This would be precisely one of the cases covered by Bacon's second *prerogative*:[1] a discovery made within the limits of the science of medicine, but arrived at experimentally, and independently of medical principles hitherto recognized. Vaccination would be another instance.'—*Op. Maj.*, vol. ii, p. 213 *n.*]

[1] [See Note F (*c*) on p. 159.]

[2] [See Note F (The Three Prerogatives of Experimental Science) on p. 157.]

EXPERIMENTAL SCIENCE

Galen had applied it in his researches into the nervous system ; Ptolemy had arrived by its means at his remarkable discovery of the refraction of light. The Arab astronomers, far more skilful mechanicians than the Greeks, had constructed extremely elaborate apparatus for the same purpose, and also to verify the equality of the angles of incidence and reflexion. But no one before Bacon had abstracted the method of experiment from the concrete problem, and had seen its bearing and importance as a universal method of research. Implicitly men of science had begun to recognize the value of experiment. What Bacon did was to make the recognition explicit. Experiment took its place as a distinct department of philosophy.

What makes this result peculiarly remarkable is that it was reached by a thinker who was so profoundly penetrated by the mathematical spirit. In this matter Roger Bacon compares favourably with his illustrious namesake of the seventeenth century, who wholly failed to appreciate the import of mathematical method. He rises to the level of one greater than either—the author of the *Discours de la Méthode*. For Descartes as for Roger Bacon, mathematics was *clavis scientiarum*, the key to the temple of science. But it was held by both alike that experiment was needed to carry out the researches which mathematical deduction had suggested; and that, as each science grew, the share taken by experiment in its progress was to become more and more predominant.[1]

XI. MORAL PHILOSOPHY

Last in order, both in the *Opus Majus* and in the *Scriptum Principale*, comes the science the study of which is the keystone and crown of the whole work—the science of life and conduct.[2] All the other sciences lead up to this. Their conclusions form its point of departure.[3]

The analysis[4] which has been given of this, as

[1] [See Note G (The Mathematical and Experimental Methods) on p. 161.]

[2] ['The seventh section of the *Opus Majus* is the crowning of the work. Its total omission from the first printed edition has entirely vitiated the popular conception of Bacon. Let us see what he says of it in the opening sentences: "I have dealt," he says, "with the study of languages, with mathematics, optics, and experimental science, and have shown how necessary they are in the pursuit of wisdom. I now proceed to a fourth science of greater value than these, the science of human conduct. We leave the region of theory, we enter the domain of practice. For though many of the foregoing sciences deal with practical operations, yet they do so in subordination to theoretical reason. This science deals with practical reason. It is the practicable science *par excellence* (*autonomatice*) which teaches us the ways of good and evil."'—*E. and A.*, pp. 185-6.]

[3] [See Note H (A Summary of Parts I-VII of the *Opus Majus*) on p. 162; also Notes C and D on pp. 151, 152.]

[4] [*i.e.* the English analysis prefixed to the Latin text of the *Op. Maj.*]

of other parts of the work, renders it unnecessary to cover the ground a second time. But a few remarks may be made on its salient features. In the first part, which treats of man's relation to God, Bacon follows the procedure common to Aquinas, indeed to most of the schoolmen, of pushing metaphysical reasoning as far as it can be made to go in support of the articles of the Catholic faith. Theology, says Aquinas (*Summa Theol.*, Pars I, quaest. i, art. 5), uses other sciences as her handmaids and assistants. Man is more easily led on to things above reason, if he begins with things which reason can demonstrate. It is true that unassisted reason is incompetent to discover and demonstrate the doctrine of the Trinity. 'Impossibile est,' he says (Quaest. xxxii, art. 1), 'per rationem naturalem ad cognitionem Trinitatis divinarum personarum pervenire.' But he goes on to explain that there are two modes of employing reason. One is to discover and prove a principle : as in physics we prove the uniformity of the motion of the heavens. The second mode is, when the principle is admitted, to show that certain observed effects are consistent with and follow from it. So, for instance, assuming the reality of our hypotheses as to eccentrics and epicycles, we can show that the movements of the planets take place in accordance with these hypotheses. It is this latter form of reasoning that we use in reference to the Trinity. 'Trinitate posita, congruunt hujusmodi rationes.' We find analogies with this doctrine when we consider what passes in our own minds. 'Ipse autem conceptus cordis de ratione sua habet quod ab alio procedat, scilicet a notitia concipientis' (Quaest. xxxiv, art. 1). 'Quanto aliquid magis intelligitur, tanto conceptio intellectualis est magis intima intelligenti, et magis unum . . . unde cum divinum intelligere sit in fine perfectionis . . . necesse est quod Verbum divinum sit perfecte unum cum eo a quo procedit, absque omni diversitate' (Quaest. xxvii, art. 1). Similarly (art. 3), the procession of the Third Person is likened to the operation of the will which we call in human beings love. 'Processio Verbi attenditur secundum actionem intelligibilem. Secundum autem operationem voluntatis invenitur in nobis quaedam alia processio, scilicet processio amoris, secundum quam amatum est in amante, sicut per conceptionem verbi res dicta vel intellecta est in intelligente. Unde et, praeter processionem Verbi, ponitur alia processio in divinis, quae est processio amoris.'[1]

[1] It is perhaps hardly necessary to refer in this connexion to Hampden's lectures on *The Scholastic Philosophy considered in its Relation to Christian Theology*. Compare p. 81 (second edition), 'The object of the Scholastic Theology was to detect

MORAL PHILOSOPHY

Bacon, as we might expect, was not less eager to find the mysteries of revelation foreshadowed by human reason. Holding, as he has fully explained in the second part of the *Opus Majus*, that the rise and progress of Greek philosophy was no less a part of divine providence than the succession of the priests and prophets of Judæa, he found without surprise that Aristotle, Plato, Porphyry, and others had apprehended, more or less dimly, some of the fundamental truths of Christian theology; among them being the Trinity, the Incarnation, the existence of angels, and the resurrection of the body. Moral philosophy, as Bacon conceived it, was in every respect concurrent with theology. 'De iisdem negotiatur quibus theologia, licet alio modo.' It is perhaps more surprising that he should have gathered these truths not merely from Greek and pre-Christian writers, but from the great Mohammedan teachers, such as Albumazar, Avicenna, and Al-Ghazali. Some of the most remarkable passages in the first part of his Moral Philosophy are quotations from Avicenna. More than once he refers to the passage in which Avicenna, speaking of future life in the unseen world, observes: 'Our present rela-

and draw forth from the Scripture, by aid of the subtle analysis of the philosophy of Aristotle, the mystical truths of God on which the Scripture Revelation was conceived to be founded.'

tion to that life is like that of the deaf man who never listened to the delights of harmony, though he never doubted that such delights existed.' Or again : 'We are like the palsied man to whom delicious food is offered which yet we cannot taste till the palsy be healed.' Avicenna tells us how the soul's vision is clogged by bodily impulses, and limited by the obtruding influences of the visible world ; and he insists on the need of purging the soul from sin, of concentration of its forces on invisible things, and of acceptance of revealed truth. We may well believe that the attempt to level up Mohammedan philosophers to the level of Christian teachers was among the *novitates* for which Jerome d'Ascoli cut short Bacon's philosophical career.

The second part of the Moral Philosophy, dealing with the laws of civil and social life, is summarily disposed of in two short chapters. Possibly a reason for this cursory treatment may be found in Bacon's aversion to the introduction of Roman law, which finds vehement expression in the twenty-fourth chapter of the *Opus Tertium*, and again in the *Compendium Studii Philosophiae* (Brewer, pp. 84-87, and 418).[1]

[1] Something additional on this subject was probably said in the missing sixth part of the *Moralis Philosophia*. But his language on the subject does not warrant the belief that the subject was fully dealt with. Cf. *Op. Tert.*, cap. xiv, Brewer, p. 52. [See the footnote to p. 138.]

We are here brought face to face with the failure, and the cause of the failure, of Bacon's social and political ideal. He was aiming at an enlarged and renovated Catholicism which should bind together and incorporate all that was best and noblest in Hebrew, Greek, and Arabic tradition in the fabric of the Christian Church, for the spiritual government of the world. The keystone of the fabric was supplied by the mistress-science, theology, resting on Mosaic and Christian revelation, consolidated by Aristotelian philosophy, and penetrated by the vital and progressive spirit of natural science. A progressive papacy, carrying on in continuous and harmonious development the work which Mosaic law and Greek intellect had begun —such was Bacon's vision:[1] and the marvellous upheaval of thought in Paris and elsewhere during the thirteenth century seemed to bring that vision within reach of fulfilment.

But while Paris was building up its systems of philosophic theology, south of the Alps, in the rival University of Bologna, work of another kind was going on. The study of the civil law of Rome, which had never wholly ceased in the cities of North Italy, had been stimulated early in the twelfth century by the teaching of Irnerius and others; and from that teaching the University of

[1] [See Note I (Bacon as a Catholic) on p. 166.]

Bologna gradually arose, as the University of Paris had arisen from the teaching of Abelard. It was a momentous event in the history of Europe. Civil law was a study as secular as the Roman empire itself. Clerical and lay students sat at the lectures side by side. 'Very early in the twelfth century men of mature age, men of good birth and good position, beneficed and dignified ecclesiastics, or sons of nobles, flocked from the remotest parts of Europe to the lecture-rooms of Bologna.'[1] The civil law embraced the entire system of man's social relations, and dealt with them on principles with which theology had no concern.

The Church felt the danger, and coped with it in the only way that was possible, by borrowing weapons from her lay rival, and arranging her own system of law in a form not less comprehensive and systematic. Irnerius had hardly finished his lectures when a fellow-citizen, the monk Gratian, in *c.* 1148 published his great text-book of canon law known as the *Decretum*, to which, in 1234, Gregory IX added five books of Decretals.

Nominally the situation was saved, but at the cost of secularizing the Church. For the canon law was in reality based on the civil law. 'Everything in the Canon Law was Roman which was

[1] [H. Rashdall, *The Universities of Europe in the Middle Ages*, vol. i, p. 124.]

MORAL PHILOSOPHY

not of directly Christian or Jewish origin.'[1] 'After the age of Gratian the studies even of ecclesiastics took a predominantly legal turn. Speculative Theology was abandoned in favour of the Canon and even of the Civil Law ; while the estrangement of the Canon Law from Theology kept pace with the increasing closeness of its union with the Faculty of Civil Law.'[2] In 1219 Honorius III formally prohibited the study of civil law in Paris on the ground that it threatened to extinguish the study of theology in the one great theological school of Europe. But prohibitions that were powerless to exclude Aristotle were equally impotent against the invasion of Ulpian and Justinian.

Bacon's pages reflect very vividly the conflict of clerical with secular influences. 'More praise,' he says, 'is gained in the Church of God by a civil jurist, though he may know nothing but civil law and be utterly ignorant of canon law and theology, than by any master in theology, and he is more quickly promoted to high ecclesiastical positions.' 'Oh that the canon law might be purged from the superfluities of civil law, and be ordered by theology,' he exclaims, 'then would the government of the Church be carried on honourably and suitably to its high position' (*Op. Tert.*, cap. 24).

[1] [Rashdall, vol. i, p. 135.] [2] [*Ibid.*, p. 138.]

He recurs to the same subject in a later work. 'For the last forty years the abuse of the civil law of Italy has been undermining not merely the study of philosophy, but the Church of God, and all the kingdoms of Christendom.' 'They monopolize,' he proceeds to say, 'every office of emolument, so that students of theology and philosophy are deprived of the means of following their studies. And besides this, the study of civil law is obliterating the distinction between clerical and lay professions. The doctors of law of Bologna call themselves clerks and masters, though they have not the tonsure, though they take to themselves wives, have families, and in every respect adopt the ways and practices of laymen. . . . If clergymen and laymen are to be subject to the same law, at least let it be the law of England for Englishmen, and of France for Frenchmen, and not the law of Lombardy' (*Comp. Stud. Phil.*, cap. 4).[1]

When Bacon appealed to the Pope to arrest the diffusion of civil law, he was like one who should attempt to stop the tide or the courses of the stars. He was fighting against the laws of historical evolution. It was written that the constitution

[1] This was written (as Brewer shows, p. lv) in 1271, three years after the death of Clement IV. Guy Fulcodi, before his ecclesiastical career began, had been a distinguished lawyer, and would hardly have tolerated such strong language.

of society should be settled on a human and secular, not on a theological basis ; and the study of civil law, radiating in the twelfth and thirteenth centuries from Bologna into every part of Christendom, was one of the most significant among many signs that the function of the Catholic Church, as the organizer of political society, was gone.

Widely different was the future of that Church in all that related to personal morality. Yet here too there was much to be desired. In the third part of the work this subject is discussed with great fullness. 'On virtue and vice,' says Bacon, 'the ancient philosophers have spoken so wonderfully that a Christian man may well be astounded at men who were unbelievers thus attaining the summits of morality.' 'On the Christian virtues of faith, hope, and charity,' he adds, 'we can speak things of which they knew nothing. But in the virtues needed for integrity of life, and for human fellowship, we are not their equals either in word or deed. Blameworthy and shameful in us that it should be so.' Acting on this view, Bacon has composed this third part almost entirely of selections from Aristotle, Plato, Cicero, and above all, from Seneca, adding the fewest words of his own that were needed to mould them into systematic shape.

He begins by adopting Aristotle's general scheme of the moral virtues as means between opposing vices. From these he passes to the consideration of special vices in the order of the seven mortal sins of Catholic theology. Six of these deal with man's conduct under prosperous circumstances; the seventh, anger, with his conduct in adversity. Dealing briefly with the first class, Bacon devotes much more attention to the subject of anger. His reason for doing so lay in the disturbing influences of this passion on the whole of man's life, public and private; and also that, in seeking remedies for its ravages, we are led up to the state of inward peace and resignation under outward trials which forms the highest plane to which the soul can aspire.

Nearly the whole of Seneca's three dialogues on Anger are quoted, but with complete rearrangement, in pursuance of the aim in view. Beginning with a picture of this passion and its disastrous effects on the highest qualities of the soul, such as clemency, pity, and joy, he enlarges on examples of self-restraint, and thence proceeds to consider remedial action; patient inquiry, time allowed for the mood to pass by, and constant remembrance of human fellowship with the offender.

This leads him to the wider subject of fortitude under calamity, of forgiveness of injury and insult,

MORAL PHILOSOPHY

of recognition of the truth that whom God loves He chastens. He concludes the section with long selections from the dialogues on consolation under bereavement, exile, and poverty, on the shortness of life and the state of inward bliss and spiritual peace. It appears that though other parts of Seneca were well known, especially the series of letters to Lucilius, these dialogues had escaped notice till Bacon called attention to them. The apocryphal correspondence between Seneca and St Paul shows that an affinity between Seneca and Christian teaching had been widely recognized in the Church. Nowhere is this affinity so strongly marked as in the dialogues *De Providentia*, *De Vita Beata*, and *De Tranquillitate Animi*, from which Bacon has quoted so largely.

The fourth part of the Moral Philosophy contains the first attempt ever made at the comparative study of the religions of the world. These Bacon ranges in six classes: Pagans, Idolaters, Tartars, Saracens, Jews, Christians. What specially called attention to this subject in Bacon's time were the events proceeding in Central Asia, and already seriously affecting European politics. Mongol hordes had swept over Russia and South Eastern Europe, and were threatening the western kingdoms. Franciscan and Dominican missionaries had been sent by Pope Innocent IV and by

Louis IX to investigate the danger at its source.[1] The reports brought back by these missionaries, especially those of Carpini and Rubruquis, brought the religious problem before the view of the leaders of the Church in all its magnitude. It was seen that beyond the Christian world, beyond the Mohammedan world which bounded it, there lay regions of unsuspected magnitude in the extreme East, where other creeds prevailed. One of these was Buddhism, recently imported into Central Asia from Tibet, with its elaborate monastic system, its image-worship, and its complicated liturgy. This creed was always spoken of by Rubruquis and Carpini, as by Marco Polo in the succeeding generation, as Idolatry. Christianity of the Nestorian type was widely disseminated; though not, it would seem, in its

[1] ['At the Council of Lyons in 1245 it was decided by Pope Innocent IV to send a mission to the Tartar Khan (Kuyuk, grandson of Chinghis). Carpini of Perugia, one of St Francis's earliest disciples, was chosen to conduct the mission. He reached the Khan's headquarters in Siberia in the following year, and he has left us a full record of his travels. Eight years afterwards a similar mission was sent by Louis IX, and entrusted to a Flemish Franciscan, Rubruk, often spoken of as Rubruquis. His account of Central Asia and its inhabitants is even more full of life and incident than Carpini's. I dwell upon these missions because of the deep impression which they made on the mind of Bacon, who makes repeated references to them in the fourth and the seventh sections of his *Opus Majus*.'—*E. and A.*, p. 169.]

MORAL PHILOSOPHY

most highly militant form. Side by side with these were tribes whose religion was of a lower grade, not rising above the rudest fetichism; these were spoken of as Pagans. Between these various modes of faith the Tartar chiefs held a doubtful and almost neutral attitude. If these could be brought within the pale of the Catholic Church, Mohammedanism, crushed between the forces of the West and the extreme East, would cease to be a danger. The issue remained undecided in Bacon's time. But we can imagine with what interest he would confer, as he tells us that he did, with Rubruquis on his return to Paris, and listen to his story of the Parliament of Religions, Saracen, Christian, and Buddhist, held at Kara Korum at the suggestion, and under the presidency, of Mangu Khan. (*Cf.* vol. ii, p. 387.)[1]

In Bacon's demonstration of the superiority of Christianity to other religions, use is made of this singular experiment. The majority of those who

[1] ['The account of this religious parliament will be found in pp. 352–360 of Rubruquis's narrative;[2] it is full of interest. There was a very large gathering of Nestorian Christians, of Mussulmans, and of Buddhists, here called Tuini, each bringing their wisest as champions. Violent or contentious language was strictly forbidden under pain of death. Three arbiters, a Christian, a Mohammedan, and a Buddhist, were appointed.'— *Op. Maj.*, vol. ii, p. 387 *n.*]

[2] [*Recueil de Voyages et de Mémoires* (Paris Geog. Soc.), t. iv, 1839.]

took part in it accepted the unity of God. The Pagans were few in number. The Buddhists (spoken of as Idolaters) raised the question of the origin of evil as an objection to a single ruler of the universe; but they allowed the question to be evaded. The Tartars, though somewhat indifferent on religious matters, were disposed to side with the Mohammedans and Christians in maintaining the unity of God. On the whole, the conclusion to which this conference tended was a fair sample, in Bacon's judgment, of the preponderating voice of mankind.

Appeal is then made to Aristotelian reasoning as to the necessity of a First Cause. The attributes of wisdom and goodness are shown to follow from omnipotence. Man's duty being to do God's will, how is man to know it? Evidently by revelation. And which revelation is true? There can be but one: for if there were more the human race could not be united. 'The unity of the Church follows from the unity of God. If there were more gods than one, more worlds than one, and more mankinds than one, then there might be more revelations than one, but not otherwise.' Which, then, is the true revelation? On a comparison of the six religions before us, three, the Pagan, the Buddhist, and the Tartar, are at once ruled out. Of the three that remain, the Jewish, the Saracen, and the Christian, philosophic reasoning, external and miraculous evidence, and ethical purity combine in giving preference to the last. The book, as we have it, closes with some ardent and rapturous words on the Sacrament of the Altar, as the means whereby Christ always remains present with His Church.

Of the two missing parts we are not left in entire ignorance. We know from the fourteenth chapter of the *Opus Tertium* that the purpose of the fifth part was to insist upon such modes of setting forth moral truth as were likely to impress, not merely the intellect, but the emotions and character of the hearer. The art of preaching, Bacon thought, was one demanding the most serious and systematic study. Rhetoric was no mere field for the gratification of vanity by ornamental display. It was a part of logic, and the most important part, since by its means truth was so conveyed to the listener that 'he is seized unawares and lifted above himself and filled with thoughts beyond his power to control, so that if evil he is absorbed by the love of good, if imperfect he receives the spirit of perfection, not through violence, but through the strong and gentle power of speech.' Rhetoric thus conceived implied the study of music in its widest sense, the study of rhythm and metre, the management of voice and of gesture (*Op. Tert.*, cap. 75).

The sixth and final part of Bacon's Moral Philosophy treated, he says, of lawsuits and of justice. He implies, however, that he dealt with this subject cursorily.[1]

XII. GENERAL CHARACTERISTICS OF THE *OPUS MAJUS*

The question presents itself: How far can the *Opus Majus*, with its two appendices, the *Opus Minus* and the *Opus Tertium*, be accepted as the final exposition of Bacon's philosophy and polity? It is spoken of by the author throughout as a *persuasio praeambula*. It is a hortatory discourse addressed to a busy statesman (for Clement IV, like most other popes of the thirteenth century, may be so called), urging him to initiate a reform of Christian education, with the direct object of establishing the ascendency of the Catholic

---

[1] [This sixth part appears never to have been written, as on p. 179 of *Un fragment inédit de l'Opus Tertium de Roger Bacon précédé d'une étude sur ce fragment par Pierre Duhem* (1909), the following statement by Bacon occurs:—'Et tandem in fine innuebam ad partem philosophie moralis ultimam, que est de causarum et controversiarum excussione, coram judice, inter partes: et excusavi me ab expositione istius partis.']

Church over all nations and religions of the world.

A fundamental principle with Bacon was that truth of whatever kind was homogeneous. 'All the sciences,' he said, 'are connected; they lend each other material aid as parts of one great whole, each doing its own work, not for itself alone, but for the other parts : as the eye guides the whole body, and the foot sustains it and leads it from place to place. As with an eye torn out, or a foot cut off, so is it with the different departments of wisdom; none can attain its proper result separately, since all are parts of one and the same complete wisdom' (*Op. Tert.*, cap. 4). Much light is thrown by passages like these, and there are many such, on the varied and at first sight heterogeneous character of the *Opus Majus*. A glance at the Index[1] of this edition will give some notion of the multiplicity of the topics treated. History of philosophy, comparative philology, mathematics, astronomy, geography, optics, the physiology of sensation, all find a place; and all are subordinated to the service of the Catholic Church as the guardian of the highest interests of man. All these topics are handled so far and in such a way as to convince the Pope, or others

[1] [*i.e.* the Index to vols. i and ii of the *Op. Maj.*]

in authority, of the width of the field to be cultivated, and of the importance of the object in view. Bacon's procedure is like that of a traveller in a new world, who brings back specimens of its produce, with the view of persuading the authorities of his country to undertake a more systematic exploration. To that further and more complete inquiry he proposed to devote the remainder of his life. He speaks of it in several passages of the present work under the title of *Scriptum Principale*. But, as we have reason to believe, of the twenty-five years of life that remained, more than half were sterilized by his imprisonment. When released, though he persevered, like Galileo, indomitably to the end, he was too old to think with his former vigour, and was capable only of such inferior work as the *Compendium Studii Theologiae*, or the Commentary on the *Secretum Secretorum*. There remain the years between 1268 and 1278. They produced the *Compendium Studii Philosophiae* (published by Brewer), the *Communia Naturalium*, the *Communia Mathematicae*, and other fragments of the *Scriptum Principale*. But, making large allowance for what may have been lost through neglect or through malignant hostility, or for what may yet remain to be discovered, the balance of probabilities indicates clearly enough

THE *OPUS MAJUS*

that the *Scriptum Principale* was never brought to completion. The *Opus Majus* remains the one work in which the central thought of Bacon is dominant from first to last ; the unity of science, and its subordination to the highest ethical purpose conceivable by man.

Another characteristic of Bacon's philosophy, to which it seems to me that sufficient attention has not yet been called, is the sense of historical continuity by which it is pervaded. Not indeed that Bacon stood alone in this respect. Comte, in a remarkable passage[1] of his appreciation of the mediæval Church, called attention, perhaps for the first time, to the awakening of the historic sense which the very constitution of that Church involved ; rising as it did from the threefold root of Roman law, Greek thought, and Hebrew theocracy. As an example of this influence, he proceeds to quote the example of Bossuet, one of the first of European thinkers to form, in however imperfect a way, a broad and definite conception of the unity of history. But the example of Roger Bacon, writing four centuries earlier, is even stronger and more startling. Two centuries before the Renaissance, he states explicitly what others may have implicitly thought, but would have shrunk from avowing even to

[1] [*Philosophie Positive*, vol. v, p. 247, ed. Littré.]

themselves, that the whole course of the intellectual development of mankind from the beginning of the world was not multiple but one, not discrete but continuous. He takes pains to synchronize the demi-gods, the heroes, and the thinkers of Greece with the kings and prophets of Judæa. In his conception, philosophy, science, and religious truth had a common origin with the patriarchs: though separated in later centuries, they pursued a parallel course in Judæa and in Greece. The growth of science, no less than the growth of religion, was a process of continuous evolution, taking place under divine guidance. It may be said that traces of such a doctrine as this may be found here and there in the early fathers, and especially in the writings of St Augustine. But a comparison of the ninth and tenth books of the *De Civitate Dei* with the second and seventh sections of the *Opus Majus*, will reveal a profound difference in the mode of treatment, even more than in the conclusions reached. What the earlier writer looks at as concessions wrung from an opponent, the later hails as the testimony of a friend. Augustine dwells on the points that separate the Christian from Porphyry and Seneca; Bacon on the points of union.

There are students of history even yet surviving

to whom the centuries following the fall of the Western Empire seem a chasm hard to pass; so that they prefer, with Vico, to conceive of an ancient civilization which has run its course, and a new cycle as beginning. For Roger Bacon the apparent breach of continuity was in great part filled up by the long series of thinkers and students who kept the torch of science alive in the Mohammedan schools of Mesopotamia and Spain. A glance at the Index[1] to this edition will show the use which Bacon made of such men as Tobit ben Korra, Al-Farabi, Alfraganus, Al-Kindi, Alhazen, Albumazar, Avicenna, Hali, and Averroes. They are spoken of, and most truly, not merely as the principal channels through which Greek philosophy and science were introduced to the Western world, but as having increased the treasure entrusted to them; a treasure which the Westerns of the thirteenth century, 'unless they are dolts and asses,' will regard it as their duty to transmit with due interest to their posterity.[2]

At the close of these introductory remarks, some attempt may be made to assign Bacon's position in the history of human thought. It

[1] [See the footnote on p. 139.]
[2] [See Note J (The Mohammedan Schools of Learning) on p. 167.]

appears on the surface that he belongs to the order of thinkers, typified by Pythagoras rather than by Aristotle, who engage in speculation, not for its own sake alone, but for the social or ethical results that are to follow. His protests against the intellectual prejudices of his time, his forecasts of an age of industry and invention, the prominence given to experiment, alike as the test of received opinion and the guide to new fields of discovery, render comparison with his great namesake of the sixteenth century unavoidable. Yet the resemblance is perhaps less striking than the contrast. Between the fiery Franciscan, doubly pledged by science and by religion to a life of poverty, impatient of prejudice, intolerant of dullness, reckless of personal fame or advancement, and the wise man of the world richly endowed with every literary gift, hampered in his philosophical achievements by a throng of dubious ambitions, there is but little in common. In wealth of words, in brilliancy of imagination, Francis Bacon was immeasurably superior. But Roger Bacon had the sounder estimate and the firmer grasp of that combination of deductive with inductive method which marks the scientific discoverer. Finally, Francis Bacon was of his time; with Roger Bacon it was far otherwise.

M. Hauréau, the historian of scholastic phil-

THE OPUS MAJUS

osophy, and also M. Renan, have suggested a parallel (or, it may be, have adopted it from Littré) between Roger Bacon and Auguste Comte. Some anticipation of the *Philosophie Positive* there assuredly is in Bacon's subordination of metaphysics to science, in his serial arrangement of the sciences, and in his avowal of a constructive purpose as the goal of speculative inquiry. But it is well not to push such comparisons too far. We shall best understand Bacon's life and work by regarding him as a progressive schoolman. Like the other great schoolmen of the thirteenth century, he set before himself the purpose of strengthening the Church in her work of moral regeneration, by surrounding her with every intellectual resource. But the forces that he brought to bear were not limited, like theirs, to the stationary dialectic of Aristotle; they were also, in great part, drawn from the progressive culture of natural and historical science. As compared with his successors of the Renaissance, his purpose was loftier; for, in urging the continuous advancement of knowledge, he had higher things than knowledge in view. His aim, pursued in no spirit of utilitarian narrowness, yet steadily concentrated on the moral progress of mankind, was, *Induire pour déduire, afin de construire.*

APPENDIX

NOTES A–J

NOTE A—ROBERT GROSSETESTE (p. 18)

GROSSETESTE [*c.* 1175–1253], the Suffolk peasant, was twenty-five years old when the century began. In Bacon's student days he was in the full vigour of manhood. The details of his early life are not very precisely known to us. We know little more than that he received his early training in the Oxford schools, for at Oxford there was already a *studium generale*; in other words, a University. Probably it was in the first year of the new century that he went to Paris, and took his master's degree. How many years he spent there we do not know; but shortly after his return we find him occupying the highest place in Oxford, as Regent of the Schools or of the Scholars, practically its Chancellor, a title which at a later date was formally bestowed on him.

Grosseteste fills so important a position in

ROBERT GROSSETESTE

Bacon's early life that it is impossible to pass him by. Putting together the various passages in which Bacon speaks of him, and these are many, we find the language used that of a grateful pupil speaking of a revered master. On two fundamental points Bacon is never tired of insisting: Grosseteste's knowledge of science, and his recognition of the value of Greek and Hebrew philology, not indeed as an instrument of mental training (that was not thought of in those days), but as the means for acquiring accurate and authentic knowledge of the Hebrew and Greek scriptures, and of the scientific works of Aristotle and the mathematicians and naturalists who followed him. In the admirable work recently published [1899] on Grosseteste by Mr F. S. Stevenson will be found (p. 49) an account of his *Compendium Scientiarum*, a classification of all departments of knowledge then explored. In point of comprehensiveness it amply justifies the statement of his great disciple. The Lord Robert Grosseteste, said Bacon, *novit scientias*, was acquainted with the sciences. Grosseteste's Compendium was not merely an Encyclopædia. Of these miscellaneous collections of knowledge there was more than one in the thirteenth century. The *De Proprietatibus rerum* of Bartholomew, for instance, had a wide circulation, and was known to Bacon. So too was the *Speculum* of Vincent of Beauvais, a work rivalling in bulk and weight that encyclopædic work of our own time which has found such favour with the managers of *The Times*. Grosseteste's researches in mathematical and physical science covered less ground than these, but were far more real and fruitful. He had profited by that great initiator of modern science early in the twelfth century, Adelard of Bath, the first translator of Euclid's geometry into Latin. Adelard had been followed later in the twelfth century, and early in the thirteenth, by a series of mathematicians, among whom Alexander Neckham, Alfred of Sershall, and John of Holywood or Halifax may be mentioned. Of the two greatest mathematicians of that time, Leonardo Fibonacci, the merchant of Pisa, and Jordan of Saxony, the second general of the Dominicans, Grosseteste probably knew nothing.

But Grosseteste was more than a mathematician. He was a great moral teacher and he was a good social reformer. We are not surprised to find in his *Compendium Scientiarum* one section devoted to ethics, for we know the attention which he gave to translations of the *Ethics* of Aristotle, and another section appropriated to agricultural and domestic economy, for on both these subjects he left us works of great historical interest, notably his Rules for the management of an estate made

ARISTOTLE AND PARIS

for the Countess of Lincoln to guard and govern her Lands and Hostel. Summing up all that we know of Grosseteste's many-sided life and work, we may be sure that so large and rich a nature counted for very much in the direction of Roger Bacon's career.—*E. and A.*, pp. 161-3.

NOTE B—ARISTOTLE AND THE UNIVERSITY OF PARIS (p. 20)

That Paris from the middle of the twelfth to the close of the thirteenth century was the principal focus of intellectual life in Europe hardly needs demonstration. Then as now it was the most international of cities; then as now it was the region in which thought was most swiftly transmuted into deed. Abelard's duel with St Bernard in 1140 had left permanent traces, which prepared the next generation of students for willing reception of the new light coming over the Pyrenees from Toledo. It was seen that the Aristotle of the Mohammedan world, the Aristotle of Avicenna and Averroes, contained a whole world of new knowledge about man, about natural history, about the constitution of the universe, of which the student of Aristotle's Logic (and nothing but his Logic had hitherto been known) had never dreamed. And now began the series of strange vicissitudes in the reputation of Aristotle described in John de Launoy's interesting book. In 1209 the study of Aristotle's *Physics* and *Metaphysics* was prohibited by the Council of Paris, and the prohibition was confirmed six years afterwards by the Papal Legate. In 1543 Peter Ramus was criminally prosecuted by the University before the Parlement of Paris for the impiety of maintaining Aristotle not to be infallible. Returning to the thirteenth century, the condemnation of Aristotle by the Papal Legate in 1215 was much mitigated by Pope Gregory IX in 1231, and by the middle of the century, at the time when Albert, Thomas Aquinas, and Bacon were in Paris, there was no longer any difficulty in studying Aristotle or his Arabian commentators. Aristotle was at the height of his legitimate power; the pedantifying process that was ultimately to explain, though not to justify, his depreciation by the second Bacon, had not yet begun, or at least was only visible to the prophetic eyes of Roger.—*E. 'and A.*, pp. 168–9.

TABLE OF THE *OPUS MAJUS*

NOTE C—TABLE OF THE SEVEN PARTS OF THE *OPUS MAJUS* (pp. 61, 122)

Part I. The Four General Causes of Human Ignorance and Error—
Undue regard to Authority, Custom, Popular Prejudice, and a False Conceit of our own Wisdom

Part II. The Close Affinity between Philosophy and Theology

Part III. The Utility of the Study of Foreign Languages

Part IV. The Utility of Mathematical Science—
Its Method and Objects—Its Uses in Astronomy, Optics, Theology, Chronology, Astrology, and the Correction of the Calendar—Geographical Treatise

Part V. Perspective or Optics—
General Principles of Vision, Physical and Mental—Direct Vision—Reflexion and Refraction

Part VI. Experimental Science—
A General Means of Investigation and Verification—Its Three Prerogatives

Part VII. Moral Philosophy—
The Final and Supreme Science—Man's Relation to God—Civic and Personal Morality—Comparative Study of Religions—Superiority of the Christian Faith

NOTE D—TABLE OF THE *SCRIPTUM PRINCIPALE*
(pp. 61, 122)
(*as planned and in part written by Bacon*)

Vol. I. Comparative Grammar and Logic—
   Corresponding in name to the divisions of the mediæval *Trivium*. (The following probably form parts of this volume: *Compendium Studii Philosophiae* and the *Grammatica Graeca*)

Vol. II. Mathematics—
   (1) Preliminary Principles (*Communia Mathematicae*)
   (2) Special Branches, corresponding in name to the divisions of the mediæval *Quadrivium* (Geometry, Arithmetic, Astronomy, and Music)

Vol. III. Natural Science—
   (1) General Principles (*Communia Naturalium*)
   (2) Perspective or Optics (probably represented by the *De Multiplicatione Specierum*)
   (3) Astronomy, including Geography and Astrology (*De Celestibus vel de Coelo et mundo*)
   (4) Barology
   (5) Alchemy (Speculative)
   (6) Agriculture
   (7) Medicine
   (8) Experimental Science

Vol. IV. Metaphysics and Morals—
   (A portion of the *Metaphysica* is known)

NOTE E—BACON'S GEOGRAPHY (pp. 36, 80)

The fourth section of the *Opus Majus* is devoted to Mathematics. . . . As the ruler of Christendom, destined soon, it was hoped, to be the spiritual governor of the whole world, the Pope should possess, said Bacon, a complete survey of his domain. He should know the precise position of every important city in the world, its distance from European centres, its latitude and longitude, its climate, the character of its population, and above all, the nature of their religion. Now much of this needful knowledge, Bacon goes on to explain, is available for us through the great astronomer and geographer Ptolemy, whose works have been preserved to us in the schools of science instituted four hundred years before by the successors of Mohammed in Bagdad, and by the offshoots of that school which in later times have been brought to Spain.

How carefully Ptolemy's *Syntaxis*, or, as Arab scholars called it, *Almagest*, and his *Geographia* founded upon it, had been studied by Bacon, the Geographical subsection of his *Opus Majus* shows clearly enough. Bacon saw very clearly that between Ptolemy's determinations of latitude and those of longitude a great distinction was to be made. To find the latitude of a place is a comparatively easy problem. All that is needed is to observe the angular distance of the sun from the zenith on the longest day of the year, the day called the summer solstice, when the sun mounts highest in the sky. When Eratosthenes of Alexandria, two centuries before Christ, observed that on the summer solstice at noon the sun shone at Syene into a deep well, that is, was directly above the observer's head, whereas at Alexandria on the same day at noon the sun was the fiftieth part of a circumference (in other words, 7° 12′) short of the zenith, it was easy to measure the distance between Syene and Alexandria, and in this way to determine the geographical length of a degree, assuming the earth to be a sphere.[1] In this way the position of places north and south of the equator was fairly well known to the Greeks, and was still better known to the Arabs, whose instruments were far more accurate than those of the Greeks.

But the case was wholly otherwise with regard

[1] ['But the uncertainty as to the Greek measures of length, and the coarseness of their astronomical instruments (independently of the fact that Alexandria and Syene are not on the same meridian), make it impossible to deduce any precise result from this observation. The Arabian instruments were better, but were obviously insufficient as a basis for solving the problem here discussed by Bacon, of the earth's magnitude.'—*Op. Maj.*, vol. i, p. 225 *n.*]

to distances east and west. This required the power of accurately measuring time; and in time-measurement the ancient world, and even the modern world, was very deficient till the seventeenth and eighteenth centuries.

Ptolemy's maps give four parallels of south latitude and twenty of north latitude. His degrees of longitude are measured along the equator, starting from Ferro in the Canary Islands, regarded as the farthest known land to the West. The positions assigned to each place depend in very few cases on accurate astronomical observations. Most of them are inferences derived from the statements made by travellers. Bacon was, I believe, the first of Western thinkers to be fully aware of their fallacy. The whole work, as he insists repeatedly, needed to be done over again by accurate astronomical survey of the known world, and especially of the Far East, which in his time was gradually coming into view. Such a survey could, Bacon observes, only be carried out (*Op. Maj.*, vol. i, p. 300) 'by papal or imperial authority, or by the help of some great king lending his aid to philosophic inquirers.'

Meantime accurate geographical information being, as considered, urgently necessary both for the study of human nature as affected by the influence of climate, and also for the spiritual government of the world, and for the direction of missions aimed at bringing barbarous nations within the pale of Christian civilization, Bacon did the best he could under the circumstances. He compiled his geographical treatise from such sources as were available, taking for his basis the mathematical geography of Ptolemy, and collating Ptolemy's conclusions with all the information he could get from Aristotle, from the Scriptures, from Pliny, from Seneca, from Jerome, Orosius, Isidore, and other writers accessible to him. But he never lost an opportunity of obtaining first-hand information from travellers who had themselves seen the countries he describes.

'Especially in the northern regions of Asia,' he says, 'I shall follow the account of Brother William, whom the Lord King Louis of France sent to the Tartars in the year of our Lord 1253. He travelled over the regions of the north and east and the lands leading to them, and he wrote of what he had seen to this illustrious king. I have carefully studied his book, and have·conversed with its author, and also with many others who have explored countries of the east and south.'[1]

Remember that all this was many years before the time of Marco Polo.—*E. and A.*, pp. 170-2.

[1] [*Op. Maj.*, vol. i, p. 305.]

NOTE F—THE THREE PREROGATIVES OF EXPERIMENTAL SCIENCE (p. 120)

(*a*) *The Three Prerogatives*

This word [*prerogative*] is used as the equivalent of *dignitas*, which is sometimes, in mediæval Latin, the translation of ἀξίωμα. 'Leading feature' will perhaps best express its meaning. In any case, these prerogatives are as follow:—

(1) Experimental science confirms conclusions to which other scientific methods already point.

(2) It reaches results which take their place in existing sciences, but which are entirely new.

(3) It creates new departments of science.

It will be seen by reference to the *Novum Organum* (lib. ii, 21), and to the note on that passage on p. 413 of Dr Fowler's edition (1878), that Francis Bacon uses the word in an entirely different sense from that intended in the *Opus Majus*. With regard to the first of Roger Bacon's *prerogatives*, a passage from Whewell (*Hist. of Induct. Sciences*, vol. i, p. 373, ed. of 1857) may be quoted. 'We may observe that by making Mathematics and Experiment the two great points of his recommendation, Bacon directed his improvement to the two essential parts of all knowledge, Ideas and Facts, and thus took the

course which the most enlightened philosophy would have suggested. He did not urge the prosecution of experiment to the comparative neglect of the existing mathematical sciences and conceptions; a fault which there is some ground for ascribing to his great namesake and successor.'
—*Op. Maj.*, vol. ii, p. 172 *n.*

(*b*) *The First Prerogative*

The foregoing chapters [on the rainbow] must be judged partly as a piece of scientific research, partly as a method; as an illustration that is of Roger Bacon's first *prerogative*, the confirmation of mathematical reasoning by experiment and observation. It will be noted that these last words are used in the widest sense; being made applicable, as the first chapter shows, to the drawing of a geometrical diagram : an extension of ordinary use which reminds us of the opening sentences of Wallis' *Arithmetica Infinitorum* (1655), in which the inductive method is frankly applied to the investigation of series.

Bacon was led by his method to some sound results. He begins with a collection of phenomena, colours in crystals or half-polished surfaces, in spray from a mill-wheel, or from an oar when lit by the sun, and the like, which, as Whewell says, ' are almost all examples of the same kind as the phenomena under consideration.' He combines astronomical theory with astronomical observation in explaining the connexion between the altitude of the bow and that of the sun. In his proof that the centre of the bow, of the eye, and of the sun are always in one straight line, the union of theory with observation is equally marked. The conclusion that each observer sees a distinct rainbow is clearly drawn. Not less striking is his discussion of the form of the rainbow ; which was pushed as far towards the truth as was possible at a time when the law of variation in the angles of refraction was still undiscovered.

With regard to the colours of the rainbow, and indeed with regard to colour in general, he shared the ignorance, not of his own time only, but of the three centuries and a half that followed, till Descartes initiated the analysis of white light into the spectrum (*Météores*, Discours huitième).—*Op. Maj.*, vol. ii, p. 201 *n.*

(*c*) *The Second Prerogative*

The second *prerogative* corresponds to the class of cases in which deductive reasoning, while not excluded, holds yet a position subordinated to experiment. An apt illustration of it is afforded by the whole career of the great physicist Faraday, who, while not denying the value of mathematical reasoning in his electrical researches, yet made no personal effort to acquire the use of this instrument, feeling, as he used to say, that it would withdraw him from his experiments.—*Op. Maj.*, vol. ii, p. 202 *n*. [For other examples see footnote on p. 120.]

(d) *The Third Prerogative*

Bacon's third *prerogative* deals with the phenomena lying outside the boundaries of any science recognized in his time, in which new departments of knowledge were to be created by experiment and observation alone. Here obviously the restraining influence of deduction from established principles could be no longer exercised; and observation unguided by rational hypothesis, led to strange results. For rules of induction, even faintly analogous to those of the *Novum Organum*, the student of the *Opus Majus* will seek in vain. Yet those who are disposed to be severe on the credulity of Roger Bacon, or of his century, will find it well matched, if not surpassed, in the *Sylva Sylvarum* of his namesake. We may go farther. His description of the mutual attraction of the split hazel-wands is curiously suggestive of the procedure followed even now by water-finders, who are not seldom consulted by practical men.

In his attempt to handle scientifically the real

MATHEMATICS AND EXPERIMENT 161

or pretended wonders exhibited by the wizards of his time, and to sift true from false, Bacon showed singular audacity as well as insight. The few physicians of our time who have striven to do the same with the allegations of clairvoyants, have had to run the gauntlet of imputations dangerous to their fame, though not, as in Bacon's case, to liberty or life.—*Op. Maj.*, vol. ii, p. 222 *n*.

NOTE G—THE MATHEMATICAL AND EXPERIMENTAL METHODS (p. 122)

It is this combination of mathematical with experimental method that marks the difference between Roger Bacon and the more famous author of the *Novum Organum*. Francis Bacon speaks of mathematics as he speaks of Aristotle, with scornful irony. Roger Bacon believes mathematics to be absolutely necessary for sound views of nature, and at the same time to be by itself utterly insufficient. Aristotle and the mathematicians, he said, may supply certain general principles of research. But their verification must be sought in special sciences (*scientia particularis*), in optics, in chemistry (*alkimia speculativa*), in the study of plants and animals (*agricultura*), and generally in experimental research. Without this the natural philosopher will be *nudus*, he says : unequipped.

His work will be a mere collection of deductions from a few abstract, remote, and undeveloped principles. (See *Op. Maj.*, vol. iii, pp. 184–5.)

Something should be said of his anticipation of the physical and mechanical discoveries of later centuries. Bacon did not invent the telescope any more than he invented the steamboat or the locomotive or the flying-machine. But his scientific imagination gave him an astonishingly clear forecast of all these things. What may be said of him is that he set the world upon the right track towards their discovery; experiment and observation combined with mathematics, when mathematics were available, and when they were not available, then experiment and observation pursued alone. Much of what he says on these things was learnt in the workshop of Peter Peregrinus.— *E. and A.*, p. 185.

Note H—A Summary of Parts I–VII of the *Opus Majus* (p. 122)

Throughout the *Opus Majus* there is an orderly arrangement of the subject-matter formed with a definite purpose, and leading up to a central theme, the consolidation of the Catholic faith as the supreme agency for the civilization and ennoblement of mankind. For this end a com-

SUMMARY OF OPUS MAJUS 163

plete renovation and reorganization of man's intellectual forces was needed. After a brief exposition of the four principal impediments to wisdom—authority, habit, prejudice, and false conceit of knowledge—Bacon proceeds in his second part to explain the inseparable connexion of philosophy with the highest truths of religion. In primæval ages both were entrusted to the patriarchs. Subsequently, while the evolution of religious truth was proceeding in Judæa, Greece became the scene of the growth of philosophy. Both were alike ordained in God's providence. In our own times, as in those of antiquity, the study of both should be carried on continuously. But for this purpose it was essential that the wisdom of the ancients should be studied in the language in which it was originally set forth. To limit students to Latin translations is to ensure the multiplication of error. Most of these translations, especially those of the Bible and of Aristotle, are deplorably defective, and have been made by men imperfectly acquainted with the subject treated of. The first condition, therefore, of a renovation of learning is the systematic study of at least three languages besides Latin, namely, Hebrew, Greek, and Arabic.

The second condition was the application of

mathematical method to all objects of study, whether in the world or in the Church. Mathematics is the 'gateway and the key to all other sciences'; it raises the understanding to the plane at which knowledge can be distinguished from ignorance. Without it other sciences are unintelligible. It reveals to us the motions of the heavenly bodies, and the laws of the propagation of force in things terrestrial, of which the propagation of light may be taken as a type; without it we are incapable of regulating the festivals of the Church; we remain in ignorance of the influences of climate upon character; of the position of cities and of the boundaries of nations whom it is the function of the Catholic Church to bring within her pale, and to control spiritually. With these subjects the fourth and fifth sections of the *Opus Majus* are occupied; they form the principal bulk of its contents. But mathematical method, though essential, is insufficient. It must be supplemented by the method of experiment. Even a purely geometrical proof is not convincing or conclusive, until the execution of the diagram has enabled us to add ocular, that is to say, experimental, evidence that the demonstration is sound. This method, moreover, will lead us into new regions into which mathematical procedure is not able

SUMMARY OF OPUS MAJUS 165

to penetrate. Experimental science governs all the preceding sciences ('domina est omnium scientiarum praecedentium'), it controls their methods; in prosecuting its own special researches it makes use of their results.

Here then ends the *Opus Majus* as presented in the edition of 1733. A glance at the fourteenth and preceding chapters of the *Opus Tertium*, in which the structure and purpose of the *Opus Majus* are reviewed, will show how disastrously the suppression of the seventh section of the work has mutilated it. 'All these foregoing sciences,' says Bacon, 'are, properly speaking, speculative. There is indeed in every science a practical side, as Avicenna teaches in the first book of his *Art of Medicine*. Nevertheless, of Moral Philosophy alone can it be said that it is in the special and autonomatic sense practical, dealing as it does with human conduct with reference to virtue and vice, beatitude and misery. All other sciences are called speculative: they are not concerned with the deeds of the present or future life affecting man's salvation or damnation. All procedures of art and of nature are directed to these moral actions, and exist on account of them. They are of no account except in that they help forward right action. Thus practical and operative sciences, as experimental alchemy and the rest, are regarded as speculative in reference to the operations with which moral or political science is concerned. This science is the mistress of every department of philosophy. It employs and controls them for the advantage of states and kingdoms. It directs the choice of men who are to study in sciences and arts for the common good. It orders all members of the state or kingdom so that none shall remain without his proper work.'—*Op. Maj.*, vol. i, pp. viii–xi.

NOTE I—BACON AS A CATHOLIC (p. 127)

Bacon's purpose, as we have seen, was to institute under papal authority a school of scientific and progressive culture that should enable the West to hold its own against the East, and thus promote the work of the Church in civilizing and evangelizing mankind. We should wholly misconceive him, such at least is my firm belief, if we supposed that his language on this matter was a veil beneath which heterodox speculation might be allowed to pass. He was not merely orthodox in the common acceptation of the word, but intensely papal. The popes of his time, and of the century before him, were great spiritual rulers ; and such harmony between the Western nations as existed was preserved by their authority. Bacon did not live to see Boniface. With the

MOHAMMEDAN SCHOOLS 167

downfall of an independent papacy in the fourteenth and fifteenth centuries a wave of barbarism and darkness swept over North-Western Europe. One of its results was the Hundred Years' War. Nobody thought then of studying Greek in Oxford, or in Paris either.

We have to look on Bacon, not as a pure speculative thinker following obscure and special lines of research for the intellectual satisfaction which they conveyed, but as an orthodox and enthusiastic Catholic, convinced that the limits of orthodoxy needed and were capable of enlargement, that Catholic truth and scientific truth were alike revelations proceeding from the same source, and converging to the same end; that scientific truth was always growing; and that the worst enemies of the human race were those who thought they possessed the whole of it.—*E. and A.*, pp. 181–2.

Note J—The Mohammedan Schools of Learning (p. 143)

Much has been said of late of what we owe to the Arabs, in other words to the Mohammedan world, in the period when scientific study was non-existent, or, if that word be too strong, at any rate non-progressive and stagnant, in the schools of Christendom. Much has been said, but I think not nearly enough.

From the institution of the school of Bagdad early in the ninth century to the capture of Bagdad by the Tartar general Houlacou in 1258, a period of more than four centuries, scientific culture was carried on throughout the East with restless energy. All that had been done by the Greeks in Arithmetic, Geometry, Astronomy, Chemistry, Natural History, the structure of the human body, became accessible in Arabic. Even now there are many sections of Galen's works that are only known to us through translations from Arabic into Latin. The best part of the work of Apollonius, the greatest after Archimedes of Greek geometers, has come to us through the same source. And it would be an utter mistake to suppose that all this Arabic learning was mere dead erudition. It was alive, and grew. The Arabic instruments of observation were more precise and accurate than those of the Greeks. We owe to them the adoption, if not the discovery, of decimal notation. Albategnius gave new life to the science of Trigonometry, and determined with nearer approach to accuracy than Hipparchus the precession of the equinoxes. Mohammed ben Musa laid the foundations of modern Algebra; Alhazen of Optics. To tell of Arabic researches in Chemistry and Medicine would need a volume.—*E. and A.*, pp. 173-4.

INDEX OF PROPER NAMES

(*References are to pages and footnotes*)

Abelard, 51, 128, 149.
Adam Marsh (de Marisco), 17, 26.
Adelard of Bath, 19 *n.*, 43, 79 *n.*, 148.
Ailly, Pierre d': *Imago Mundi*, 36.
Albategnius, 168.
Albertus Magnus, 11, 12, 24, 34, 46, 55, 83 *n.*; *De Coelo*, 53; *Metaph.*, 51; *Summa theol.*, 45.
Albumazar, 89, 125, 143.
Alexander Neckham, 19, 44, 148.
of Hales, 11, 20, 32, 34, 55; *Summa univ. theol.*, 24.
Alexandrian School, 43.
Al-Farabi: *see* Farabi.
Alfraganus, 143.
Alfred (Alured) the Englishman, 70.
Al-Ghazali: *see* Ghazali.
Alhazen, 143, 168; *Thesaurus Opticae*, 38-9, 99 *n.*, 102, 104-8.
Al-Khwarizmi: *see* Mohammed ben Musa.
Al-Kindi: *see* Kindi.
Al-Mamun, 79.
Amalric (Amaury) of Bena, 45, 49.

Andrew the Jew, 71 and *n.*
Antoninus, St: *Summa Hist.*, 12.
Apollonius, 75, 82, 168.
Aquila, 68.
Aquinas, St Thomas, 11, 12, 34, 55, 72, 83 *n.*; *De universal.*, 51; *Summa theol.*, 53, 86-8, 123-4.
Arabic, 43 and *n.*, 62, 63, 168.
Arabs, The, 43, 104, 105 *n.*, 121, 125, 143, 153, 167-8.
Archimedes, 75, 168.
Aristotle, Aristotelian, 31, 43, 51, 69-73, 89, 98 *n.*, 125, 127, 136, 145, 149-50; *De anima*, 88, 99; *De divinat. per somnum*, 94; *De vegetab.* (spurious), 59; *Ethics*, 72, 131-2, 148; *Metaph.*, 19, 46, 49, 69 *n.*; *Meteorol.*, 70; *Organon*, 69, 149; *Physics*, 19, 46, 69 *n.*, 93 *n.*; *Poetics*, 72; *Rhetoric*, 72.
Augustine, St, 69; *De civitate Dei*, 142.
Avendeath, John, 43.
Averroes, 46, 49, 143.
Avicenna, 89, 119, 125-6, 143; *Canon medicinae*, 165; *De animalibus*, 71.

Bacon, Francis, 93, 116, 121, 144, 150, 161; *Cog. et Visa*, 40; *Nov. Org.*, 39, 100, 157-8, 160; *Sylva Sylvarum*, 160.
Bacon, Robert, 15.
[1] Bacon, Roger: *Scriptum Principale*, 28, 29, 35, 54–62, 76, 122, 140, 152; *Op. Maj.* (ed. Bridges), 5, 6–7, 13–14, 41, 61, 75, 76, 83 *n.*, 138–43, 151, 162–6; *Op. Maj.* (ed. Jebb), 5, 40, 71 *n.*; *Op. Min.*, 13–14, 76, 83 *n.*, 113 and *n.*, 138; *Op. Tert.* (ed. Brewer), 13–14, 28, 41, 76, 138, 165; *Op. Tert.* (ed. Duhem), 113 *n.*, 138 *n.*; *Op. Tert.* (ed. Little), 83 *n.*; *Comm. Math.*, 77–83, 140, 152; *Comm. Nat.*, 42, 47, 57, 78 *n.*, 140, 152; *Comp. Stud. Phil.*, 29, 140, 152; *Comp. Stud. Theol.*, 35, 140; *De alchemia* (ed. Duhem), 113 *n.*; *De astrologia* (ed. Bridges), 83 *n.*; *De celestibus*, 57 *n.*, 152; *De mult. Spec.*, 27–8, 57 *n.*, 93, 96–101, 152; *De retard. senec. accident.*, 113 *n.*, 119; *De secretis op. nat.*, 113 *n.*, 117; *Geographia*, 36, 151, 153–6; *Grammatica Graeca*, 64–6, 152; *Metaph.*, 54 *n.*, 152; *Moralis phil.*, 5, 122–38, 142, 151, 165–6; *Perspectiva*, 38–40, 101, 107–11, 151; *Sanioris Med.*, 113 *n.*; *Scientia Experiment.*, 60–1, 120–2, 151, 157–62, 164–5; *Speculum alchemiae*, 113 *n.*
Bartholomew Anglicus: *De proprietatibus rerum*, 147.
Bernard, St, 149.
Bernoulli, Daniel, 111 *n.*
Berthelot, M. P. E.: *Chimie au moyen âge*, 117 *n.*
Bible, The, 33, 66–9.
Boethius, 69 *n.*
Bologna, University of, 127–8, 131.
Bonaventura, St, 26, 53.
Boniface VIII, 166.
Bossuet: *Discours sur l'histoire universelle*, 141.
Brewer, J. S.: *Op. Ined.*, 73.
Buddhism, 134, 135, 136.
Bungay, Thomas of, 17.

Calendar, Julian, 37–8, 151.
Campanella, T., 93.
Campanus of Novara, 75.
Canon Law, 128–9.
Cantor, M.: *Gesch. der Math.*, 43 *n.*, 79 *n.*, 80 *n.*, 105.
Carpini, 134 and *n.*
Catholic Church, The, 20, 30, 127–31, 138, 139, 141, 145, 162, 164, 166–7.
Charles, Émile: *Roger Bacon*, 41.
Christianity, 133–7.
Cicero, 89, 131.
Civil (Roman) Law, 126, 127–31, 141.
Clement IV, 13 *n.*, 16, 27, 29 and *n.*, 76, 130 *n.*, 138.
V, 73.
Columbus, 36.
Combach, 39.

[1] For full bibliographical details as to the various MSS. and published works of Bacon, see Mr Little's appendix to Dr Rashdall's edition of the *Compendium Studii Theologiae* (Brit. Soc. of Franciscan Studies, vol. iii, 1911).

INDEX OF PROPER NAMES

Comte, Auguste, 7, 83 *n.* ; *Phil. Pos.*, 92 *n.*, 111 *n.*, 113 *n.*, 141, 145.
Copernicus, 38, 93.
Council of Lyons (1st), 134 *n.*
of Vienne, 73–4.

Dante : *Commedia*, 38 *n.*, 85.
David of Dinant, 45, 49.
Dee, John, 37–8, 40.
Delambre : *Hist. de l'astron. anc.*, 103 *n.*
Democritus, 94, 98.
Descartes, 98 *n.*, 121 ; *Dioptrique*, 40, 107, 110 *n.* ; *Météores*, 159.
Dominican Order, The, 34, 67.
Donatus, 62.
Duns Scotus, 36, 51, 55, 56 *n.*, 74.

Edmund Rich, 17, 26.
Elixir vitae, 115, 119 *n.*
Epicurus, 94, 95, 96.
Erasmus, 26, 75 *n.*
Eratosthenes, 154.
Euclid : *Catoptrica*, 102 ; *Elements*, 19 *n.*, 75 ; *Optica*, 102.

Farabi, 32, 143.
Faraday, 98 *n.*, 159–60.
Fleury, C. : *Hist. ecclés.*, 73.
Fox, Richard, 75 *n.*
Francis of Assisi, St, 32.
Franciscan Order, The, 11–12, 18, 26–7, 31, 32–3, 35, 67.
Frederic II (Emperor), 69, 70.

Galen, 43, 119, 121, 168.
Galileo, 34, 39, 83, 140.
Geber, 117 *n.*
Gerard of Cremona, 43, 70, 104.
Ghazali, 32, 125.

Gilbert : *De magnete*, 23–4.
Gratian (canonist): *Decretum*, 128.
Greek, 26, 43 *n.*, 62, 64–6, 75 *n.*, 147.
Greeks, The, 101, 120–1, 125, 142, 143, 168.
Gregory IX, 128, 150.
Grosseteste, Robert, 17–18, 26, 37 *n.*, 62, 72, 146–9 ; *Comp. Scient.*, 147–8 ; *De physicis, etc.*, 18.
Gundisalvi, Dominicus, 43.

Hali (physician), 119, 143.
Hampden, R. D. : *Scholastic Phil.*, 124 *n.*
Hauréau : *Hist. de la phil. scolast.*, 42, 46 *n.*, 56 *n.*, 144–5.
Hebrew, 62, 64, 147.
Heiberg, Prof. J. L., 102 *n.*
Henry of Ghent, 55.
Henry III (of England), 14–16.
Hermann the German, 17, 70, 71–2.
Hipparchus, 168.
Holywood, John (Johannes de Sacro Bosco), 148.
Honorius III, 129.
Humboldt, A. von : *Cosmos*, 36 *n.* ; *Examen de l'hist. de la géog.*, 36 *n.*
Hundred Years' War, 167.

Innocent III, 45.
IV, 134 *n.*
Irnerius, 127–8.
Isidore of Seville, 156.

Jebb, S., 5, 71 *n.*
Jerome d'Ascoli, 31, 35, 126.
St, 68–9, 156.

Jews, The, 127, 133, 137, 141, 142.
John (Roger Bacon's pupil), 29, 113 *n.*
  de Basingstoke, 17.
  of Salisbury : *Policraticus*, 42.
  Peckham, 17.
Jordan of Saxony, 79, 148 ; *De ponderibus*, 112.
Josephus, 67.
Jourdain, A.: *Recherches critiques, etc.*, 43 *n.*
Julian Calendar : *see* Calendar.
Justinian, 129.

Kepler, 93.
Kindi, 70, 99 *n.*, 104, 143.

Latin, 43 and *n.*, 62–3, 163.
Launoy, Jean de : *De varia Aristot., etc.*, 46 *n.*, 150.
Lavoisier, 114.
Leonardo of Pisa, 148 ; *Liber abaci*, 80.
Littré, 145.
Louis IX (St Louis), 134 *n.*, 156.
Lucretius : *De rerum natura*, 94, 95–6, 98.

Mangu Khan (Mongol emperor), 135.
Marsh : *see* Adam.
Martin, J. P.: *La Vulgate Latine, etc.*, 67.
Matthew Paris : *Hist. Maj.*, 14.
Michael Scot, 70–1.
Mohammed ben Musa, 79 and *n.*, 168.
Mohammedan Schools : *see* Arabs.
Mohammedanism, 133, 135 and *n.*, 136.

Neckham : *see* Alexander.
Nestorians, The, 134, 135 *n.*
Newton, 98 *n.*
Nicholas IV : *see* Jerome d'Ascoli.

Occam, William of, 51, 74.
Orosius, 156.
Oxford, University of, 18, 26, 35, 74, 75 *n.*, 146.

Pagans, 133, 135, 136.
Papacy, The, 26, 127, 166–7.
Paris, University of, 18–20, 32–3, 127, 128, 129, 149–50.
Parliament of Religions, 135.
Pastoureaux, The, 26.
Paul, St, 133.
Paul of Middelburg, 38.
Peckham, John : *see* John.
Peregrinus, Petrus, 21–4, 39, 162.
Plato, 51, 89, 125, 131.
Pliny, 89, 156.
Polo, Marco, 134, 156.
Porphyry, 125, 142.
Priestley, 114.
Priscian, 62.
Ptolemy : *Almagest (Syntaxis)*, 38 *n.*, 43, 104, 153 ; *Geographia*, 36 *n.*, 153–6 ; *Optica*, 103–4.
Pythagoras, 103, 144.

Quadrivium, The, 20, 61, 152.

Ramus, Petrus, 150.
Rashdall, Hastings : *Univ. of Europe in Middle Ages*, 74, 128, 129.
Raymond (Archbishop of Toledo), 19, 43 and *n.*
Religions, Parliament of : *see* Parliament.
Renaissance, The, 36, 40, 141, 145.

INDEX OF PROPER NAMES 173

Renan, E., 145.
Roemer, O., 99 *n*.
Roman Empire, 143.
Röntgen, W. K., 101 and *n*.
Roscellinus, 51.
Rubruquis, William of, 134-5, 156.

Saracens, The, 133.
Scholasticism and Scholastics, 19-20, 24, 30-1, 33-4, 41-56, 74, 123-4, 145.
Scot: *see* Michael.
Seneca, 142, 156; *Dialogues*, 131, 132-3.
Sershall, Alfred of, 44, 148.
Snell, W., 107.
Socrates, 33-4.
Spencer, Herbert, 92 *n*.
Stevenson, F. S.: *R. Grosseteste*, 37 *n*., 147.
Stoics, The, 32.
Symmachus, 68.

Tartars, The, 133-6.
Theodotion, 68.
Theon of Alexandria, 101, 102.
Thomas Wallensis (Bishop of St Davids), 17.

Thompson, S. P.: *Petrus Peregrinus, etc.*, 24 *n*.
Tobit ben Korra, 143.
Toledo, Schools of, 43 and *n*., 69, 149.
Toscanelli, Paolo, 36 *n*.
Trivium, The, 62, 152.

Ulpian, 129.

Vico, 143.
Vincent of Beauvais: *Speculum*, 148.
Vitello: *Optica*, 106 *n*., 107, 108 and *n*.

Wallis, John: *Arithmetica Infinitorum*, 158.
Whewell, W.: *Hist. of Ind. Sciences*, 157, 158.
William of Auvergne, 20, 25.
— of Ockham: *see* Occam.
— Rubruquis: *see* Rubruquis.
— the Fleming, 70, 72.
Witelo: *see* Vitello.
Wood Brown, J.: *Life and Legend of Michael Scot*, 71 *n*.

Young, Thomas, 98 *n*.